Newcastle's Town Moor Fair

Paul Lanagan

BOOKS OF THE NORTH

Above & Page 3: Comparative southward views of the fairground in 1949 and 2003. The modern view was taken from the Giant Wheel owned by Dutch showmen Jan Vallentgoed and Nico Buwalda. Note the similar layouts but contrasting changes, for example, the types of transport. Newcastle's horizon has changed considerably over the 54 years between the photographs.

Page 6: A lighthouse slip (helter skelter) stands proud at the Town Moor Fair in 1934. As can be seen, the showground was some distance from the Great North Road.

Newcastle's Town Moor Fair

First published in 2010 by Books of the North
ISBN-13: 978-0-9555059-0-4

British Library Cataloguing in Publication Data.
A catalogue record for this book is available from the British Library.

www.newcastle-hoppings.co.uk

CONTENTS

FOREWORD

MY VERY FIRST memory of the Hoppings is of walking there with my parents. I think that I must have been about five years old, so the year would have been 1937 or thereabouts. At that time I had four older brothers and a younger sister. We lived in a downstairs flat, near Heaton Park. My mother's chief method of keeping us in check was by taking us for long walks through Heaton Park, Armstrong Park and Jesmond Dene; after which we didn't have the energy to misbehave. The walks would vary from time to time. During Race Week a favourite change would be to walk to the Hoppings – a distance of perhaps two miles.

Surprisingly, I have no recollection of any of us going on one of the rides. We certainly looked around, because I can recall the sight, sound and smell of metal-tyred traction engines; and the steam yachts. I remember Dad buying each of us a halfpenny ice-cream cornet, while he and mother had an ice-cream sandwich. Father was a bricklayer, when jobs were available, and we were told that there was no money for anything else. So why did we bother going in the first place? Well, because if you are born in Geordieland, that is one of the things you do when you are young. It was then, and is now, a free spectacular if your pockets are empty.

In 1958, I was lucky enough to get a job as a Building Inspector with Newcastle City Council. My boss, Fred Didsbury, said to me in the following May, "Albert! I want you to give me a hand to set out the Town Moor Fair!" "What has a Building Inspector got to do with that?" I asked. He told me that it was part of his job as Chief Building Surveyor to mark out the public aisles, and the positions of the attractions. I have never understood the logic myself, so when asked, I have always replied that he was the only one who had a tape measure! It was no great shock to my system, therefore, when in 1988 I became Chief Building Surveyor, and inherited the job of marking out the Fair. Paul Lanagan is to be commended for the work and commitment that he has put into this book. The Hoppings is as much a part of Geordieland as brown ale and stottie cakes. It's in your blood!

Albert Austin
Fairground Surveyor & Former Fair Manager

INTRODUCTION

MY EARLIEST MEMORIES of the Newcastle upon Tyne Hoppings date from the early 1980s, when I was taken to see the Wall of Death motorcycle stunt show and Ron Taylor's wrestling and boxing booth, the Excelsior Pavilion, by my grandfather who had wrestled and refereed for Ron. As a small child I was terrified that the roaring motorbikes would come over the top of the cylindrical wall and I had to be taken out! Fortunately we had been allowed in free of charge. I can then recall being taken to see George the Gentle Giant, Scotland's tallest living man at 7 feet 3 inches in height. My arms barely wrapped around one of his enormous legs!

I started my serious research into the history of the Hoppings at 3.50am on Sunday June 15th 2003 on the deserted Town Moor. I gathered photos of the empty fields and cows before the long line of fairground rides, trailers, kiosks and living wagons started to arrive. Several hours later I spotted a man with a tape measure, pottering around in the long grass of the Moor. Curiosity got the better of me and I went and said hello, only to discover that I had just established contact with a very important person in the history of the Hoppings, and one who would prove to be helpful beyond belief with my research. That man was Fairground Surveyor Albert Austin.

The mass arrival of showmen lasted the entire day, and it being so hot, I soon dozed off for a nap in the long grass of the Moor. I spent the following two weeks being introduced to showmen from all around the country, as well as renewing acquaintances with the showmen I had met while researching for my first book on Houghton Feast, an ancient festival (and fairground) in Houghton-le-Spring, Co Durham.

Several years and Hoppings later, I have now come to look upon the Town Moor Fair as a temporary town. With its familiar layout, aisles and rows, I can now find my way around, even late at night, safe in the knowledge that I am surrounded by many familiar faces. This book is by no means a definitive history and is more of an insight and tribute to the dedicated people who make the biggest travelling fairground in Europe the best fairground in the world.

Paul Lanagan

ACKNOWLEDGEMENTS

THIS BOOK IS dedicated to Albert and Maureen Austin, two heroes of the Hoppings, for their enthusiasm and generosity. Without their help and support, this book would be a mere shadow of itself, and I will be forever grateful to them both. My gratitude is given to my wife Lyndsay and children Adonia, Sabaean, and Romalli, for allowing me to dedicate time to another of my projects. My sincere thanks go to Millie Barrass for showing me what happens after the lights go out and for the lifts home from the Moor, and to Joan Lambton for proofreading services.

A special thank you is extended to John Murphy and Colin Noble of the Northern Syndicate; to Thomas Dixon and Mark McCormick, two friends of the fairground; and to Dr Vanessa Toulmin and Ian Trowell of the National Fairground Archive.

For co-operation and assistance, thanks are given to: Susan Stokel-Walker and Peter Scott of Newcastle City Council; Stephen Smith of the Fairground Society; Paul Castrey of Beamish Museum; Newcastle City Library; and Tyne & Wear Archives Service.

I would also like to thank the following for their precious time and help, and I apologise to anyone I may have missed: Vira Allison; Diane Barlow; Barry the King of Guessers; Eddy Bensley; Elizabeth Bensley; Steve Barratts; Maureen Bowman; Jeff Brown; John Brown; Jan Buglass; Nan Cadman; Margaret Carter; Trevor Cartner; Gilbert Chadwick Snr; Stella Clews; Alan J. Codona; Phillip Cooper Snr; Phillip Cooper Jnr; John Coulson; Alan A. Cowie; Jo Dean; Sarah Edgar; Sir Leonard Fenwick; Allison Freeman; Billy Freeman; Rory Freeman; Katie Gascoigne; Pauline Gashinski; Bob Gladwin; Brett Graham; Michael Grieve; George Robert Hanley; Juliana Heron; Frank Howard; Rosie Ilett; Allan Jones; David Jones; Nick Laister; Richard & Irene Lanagan; Arthur Lawrence; Kathleen Lee; Melanie Lewis; Ruth Lewis; David Little; Alasdair MacKenzie; Beverly Manders; Lynn McNeany; Jake Messham; James Messham; Junior Messham; Colin Milan; Ian & Freda Miller; Arthur Robert Moody; Valerie Moody M.B.E.; John A. Moreels M.B.E.; Peter Morran; Chris Morrison; Sarah Mulligan; John Murphy Jnr; Walter Murphy; Arthur Newsome; Lisa Newsome; Colin Noble Jnr; Darren Noble; Lesley Noble; Brian O'Brien; Claire O'Brien; Sandra O'Brien; Malcolm Osbourn; Garry Overs; Alan Proudlock; Sydney Proudlock; Peggy Punton; Sheila Quigley; Bebe Ratcliffe; Kenneth Reader; Mike Reed; Denise Robertson; Joseph Robson; Rowland Scott; Kevin Scrivens; Ann Shaw; Zarra Sheeran; Sarah Sherwood; Christopher Slater; Frankie Smith; Kookie Smith; Paul Smith; Paul Stevens; Graham Stickings; Lewis Stokes; Harold Thorne; Keith Turner & Sons; Lana Turner; Alfred Twilley; Brian Usher; William Wassell; John Wilkins; Michele Wheatley; and PC David Woodward.

CHAPTER I

Temperance Festival to Town Moor Fair

Heaving! Crowds of thousands at the Temperance Festival at the turn of the century. Note the folk taking shelter from the summer sun in the shade cast by J. Ling's High Flyers in the foreground.

NEWCASTLE UPON TYNE is one of the main cities in the north of England. Near to the centre of the city is a large area of open space known as the Town Moor. The dual control of this huge expanse – about 1,000 acres of grassland – is in the hands of the City Council (formerly the Corporation), which owns the freehold, with grazing rights belonging to the Stewards' Committee of the Freemen of Newcastle upon Tyne. The actual area named 'Town Moor' comprises of about 330 acres, with the fairground now covering around 40 acres. The following article, from a 1953 volume of the Geographical Magazine, explains the origins of the fairground as a Temperance Festival in 1882 through to the fairs of the 1950s when use of the name 'Hoppings' became more common:

On the social side the Moor has been a centre for sports, exhibitions, fairs and races. It was the yearly race meeting that produced the present annual fair which has so frequently been described as "the greatest show on earth." This yearly fair is certainly a spectacle, and the word colossal is no exaggeration when applied to the gathering that assembles on the Moor every Race Week. The scene is so brilliant and so full of life that anyone interested in sociology will want to know more about its origin and history.

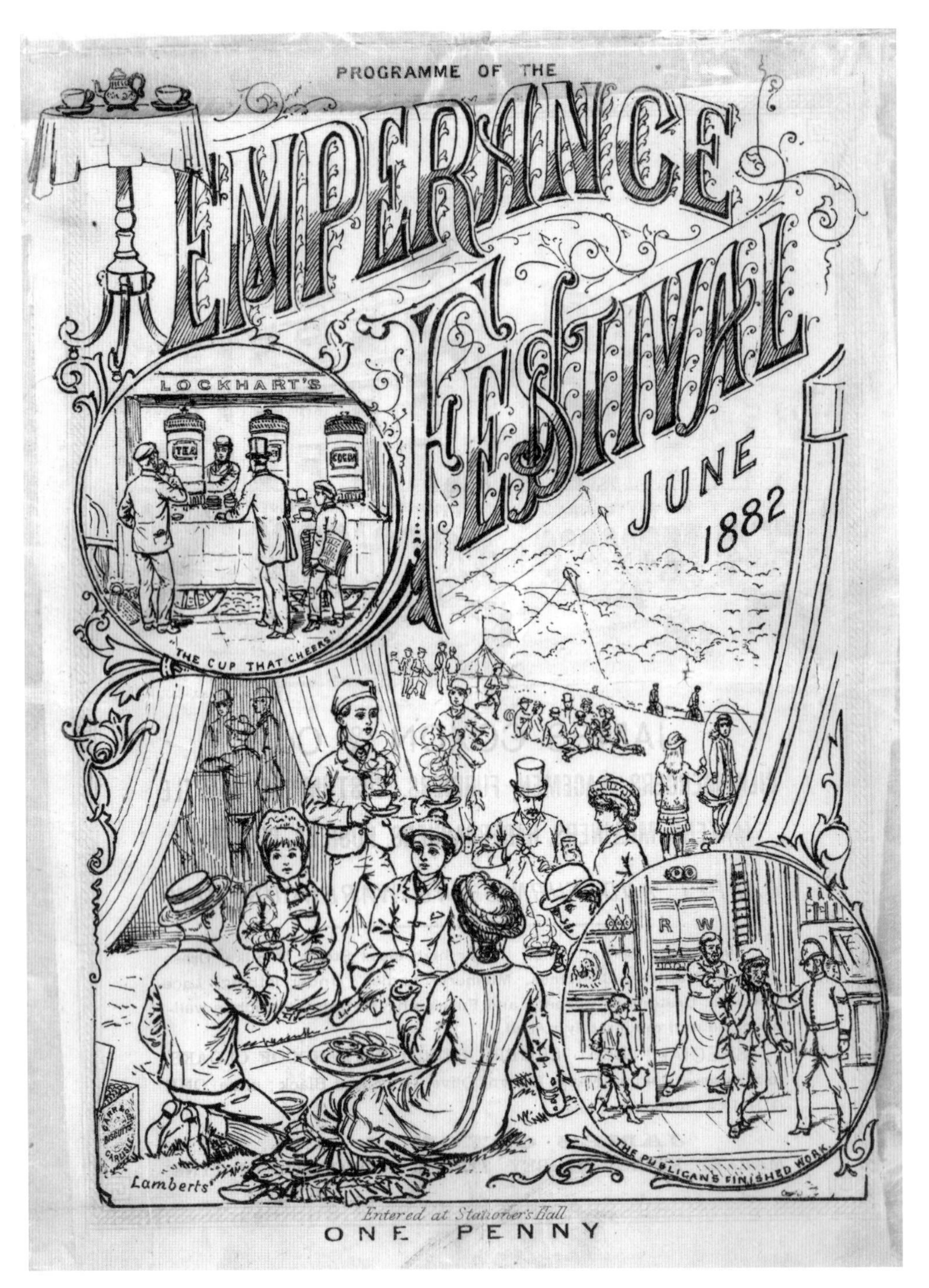

The cover of the first North of England Temperance Festival Association programme from 1882. These brochures were produced annually until the 1920s, and contained information about the proceedings, shows, sports, names of the members and officials from the Festival Committee, as well as pro-temperance messages.

Before the 17th century there is evidence that horse races were held in many parts of Northumberland, but from 1632 – 1720 they were held only at Killingworth, about six miles to the north of Newcastle. In 1721 the annual meeting was fixed for Whitsuntide and transferred to the Town Moor; thirty years later the date was changed to coincide with Midsummer Day. The meetings became exceedingly popular with dancing, cock fighting and revelry of all types providing a feast of entertainment. One feature was the meeting of friends who had been scattered far and wide – they all tried to meet once a year at "the Races." In 1881 the races were run on the Moor for the last time; and when the next year they were transferred to Gosforth Park, two miles away, it was expected that festivities on the Moor would be killed. However, by a strange twist of fate, events were conspiring to make them bigger than ever.

In the 1870s the Newcastle temperance organisations had been holding annual gatherings on various parts of Tyneside, but these had evidently been discontinued, for in 1881 there was a suggestion that they should be revived. The proposal was that meetings should be held during Race Week in three different parts of Newcastle. Plans were proceeding when, in March 1882, a letter appeared in the local press suggesting that the meetings should take place on the Moor and should be combined with festivities so as to maintain the tradition of a yearly gathering. Among other things the writer thought it would prevent the dangerous practice of taking crowds of young children away on railway excursions.

The festival proved a great success and was supported by many organisations including the YMCA, the Temperance Society, and the Gospel Society. The Newcastle Courant reported that there was a goodly collection of sports, with cycle-races, brass band contests, football, cricket, children's games and treats, and military shows. In addition, the proprietors of the many fairground shows (including high fliers and galvanic batteries) did a roaring business. There were no cardsharpers, no gambling booths, and few people under the influence of drink. The crowd, estimated at 150,000 was well behaved, an improvement on previous years. The only disappointment was the absence of wind which prevented the kite contest from being held.

The Executive Committee of the first Temperance Festival, 1882. Pictured fifth from left is Alderman W. D. Stephens, the President of the Temperance Association.

This success was a great encouragement to the promoters and it was decided to repeat the festival the following year. The 1883 gathering was on a bigger scale but was spoilt by rain. Even so it was estimated that 100,000 visited it each day. And so the festival became an annual event. In 1892 it coincided with an election campaign. The Temperance speakers at the fair urged no-one to vote for any brewer, distiller or liquor seller, and 841 sermons were preached in local churches in connection with temperance.

In 1902 the fair was twenty-one and coincided with the Coronation holiday – although the Coronation was postponed because of the King's illness. There was a new record in takings and the Newcastle Weekly Chronicle reported:

There were children and patriarchs, young and middle-aged, rich and poor, silks and satins, and miserable rags, a motley throng with one common object - a whole hearted abandonment to pleasure. The shows were going merrily. Rifles cracked at the shooting galleries, there was a perfect cannonading of balls in the coconut alleys, daintily dressed maidens flaunted their finery dancing on the platform in front of shows, burly boxers flourished the gloves before the eyes of an amazing multitude, roundabouts circled in bewildering beauty, boats swung high in the air, trumpets sounded, drums thundered, there was shouting and laughter, singing and whistling, more noises than prevailed in babel, more confusion almost than in chaos.

It was estimated in 1912 that during the thirty years some 15,000,000 people had visited the annual three-day festival. During World War I the fair was not held, but in 1919 it appeared again in all its glory to celebrate the victory of the Allies.

The 1920s and 1930s were times of industrial depression, but this did not seem to affect the size of the fair – the 1931 festival covered thirty-five acres and collected rents of £3,500 as compared with £1,000 in 1924. Estimates put the attendance at 1,000,000 each year. The fair continued through World War II and played a great part in contributing to the "holidays at home" campaign. A dispute over rents in 1946 reduced its size but the next year saw it back in full strength. And so it has continued to the present day.

So much for the history. It is, however, impossible to gain a realistic impression without a closer study of recent gatherings. The 1951-2 fairs covered some fifty acres and were about three-quarters of a mile long. Altogether about five hundred shows were assembled in five long rows. The centre row consisted of about forty of the huge mechanical devices – the moon-rockets, chair-o-planes, dodgems, octopuses, speedways, loopers and whips.

By the side of these stood the lorries and trailers with their diesel generating sets roaring away. On both sides of the centre was a row of about a hundred side-shows – housey housey, darts and penny-rolling predominating. Finally, making up the outer rows were two long lines of side-shows, again about a hundred each. These included shooting ranges, shies, automatic machines, ball-rolling games and mechanical competitions.

Some forty of these shows consisted of exhibitions – the Flea Circus, Fat Lady, Call of the West, Wall of Death, boxing, circus, vampire, freaks, the squid, and the show marked "naughty but nice". Several of these shows claimed to be straight from London, the Continent or the United States, while others claimed to be the talk of London or the talk of the town.

Jack Hammond's Gallopers at the north end of the Town Moor Fair in 1959.

Scattered round the outside were about a thousand caravans, trailers and lorries belonging to the showmen, while amongst the shows were many selling chips, pies, fruit, ice cream, balloons, hats and toys. Many one-man concerns offered to take your photograph, guess your weight (with X-ray eyes), and tell your fortune. From the moment the shows arrive crowds gather to watch the various stages of construction, and when the fair opens on the Saturday a huge multitude swarms over the whole area. The noise of the loudspeakers, the diesel engines and the fast-moving machinery make it difficult to speak, and the appetising smell of fried potatoes and the heavy sickly smell of diesel fumes mix (if the day is hot) with the dust that rises thickly. On the Sunday the huge machine is quiet but many still wander round, and on Sunday evening the whole area becomes a meeting place (on a far greater scale than Hyde Park) for political parties and religious groups.

For the next six days the festival continues with great crowds, as even today most Tynesiders have some time off during this week. The whole gigantic spectacle cannot be seen quickly – it is essential to move slowly, to stand with the crowds, to rest and absorb the brilliant scene, and to ponder on the sight of humanity in the mass. Above all it is necessary to join in the fun. With a few whirls on the Whip, the Caterpillar, or the Octopus, the blood begins to tingle and there is a feeling of excitement. Caution is thrown to the winds and it is a strange person indeed who does not spend a good deal more than he intended. At night an estimated 100,000 lights give enchantment to the scene and send a glow into the sky that can be seen for miles. On the last day prices rise, but this does not stop the crowds, and the final evening is perhaps the best time of all with the dense throng continuing well after midnight. Everyone seems to enjoy this moment to the full. The great gathering is about to end. There is a touch of sadness in the air. But nothing can quench the feeling that this festival provides one of mankind's great moments and that it is good to have seen it. It would indeed take a great deal to convince you that anyone could put up a bigger or a more light-hearted spectacle.

AN ODE TO NEWCASTLE TOWN MOOR

Every year in June time
There drops a mystic spell.
It's called Town Moor Fever,
And showmen know it well.

It hits at everybody,
From three to eighty-four
It buzzes all around us –
We must get to the Moor.

Everything gets cleaned up.
Beneath the mystic spell,
Schools and jobs and illnesses,
All just go to hell.

We pull onto the Moor,
And find our piece of land,
Beds and baby-sitters
Are in great demand.

Get built up tomorrow,
A dance tomorrow night.
We'll have to find the lampman
We've got to get some light.

Now everything is ready,
We're waiting for the Mayor,
To walk around the Moor,
And open up the fair.

Well that's the first night over.
We wonder "what's in store".
The young 'uns rush up to the path
That's what they've waited for.

Dancing on the dodgems,
Capers on the path,
John what's-his-name from Yorkshire,
He really is a laugh.

Creeping in at five o'clock
People think we're mad.
I'll have to be dead quiet
Or I'll cop one from my Dad.

The Moor lessees won't like it,
This is Dad's old cry,
But the lessees used to caper
On the Moor in days gone by.

Me granny used to caper,
And so did Mam and Dad.
The tales I've heard about him,
He really was a lad.

Crawl out of bed next morning,
Drawn and bleary eyed.
Got to get some diesel,
Do some jobs outside.

Washed and changed for 12 o'clock,
Now I'm really tired.
Minding stalls like robots,
Doing jobs with strain,
Come to life at midnight,
And do it all again.

Chasing after swagmen,
Lighting set breaks down,
Got lit up from neighbours,
Got to dash down town.

Searching for the butcher –
Wonder where he's hid.
Just have to fry some bacon.
Now we've lost the kids.

Mud and rainy weather
Windy through the night.
Get up and tie the tilts down,
See everything's all right.

Well that's the Moor over.
That fortnight has really fled.
I'm glad that it is over,
I'm just about half dead.

Looking around the Moor
As far as one can see,
Brown and baldy patches,
Where green grass used to be.

Litter strewn all over,
It's really hard to bear.
Still it will be green again
When we come back next year.

Amelia Twilley

CHAPTER II

Two Weeks in June

The Town Moor is home to grazing cattle and a popular location for dog-walkers and joggers. The land is owned by the City Council and herbage rights belong to the Freemen of Newcastle upon Tyne.

THE MODERN DAY Hoppings fairground involves around 600 show-families and 2,000 people. Contrary to popular belief, the Hoppings does not simply appear on the Town Moor overnight, with the showmen knowing exactly where to build up the rides. The operation involves many months of planning and the photographs in this chapter give an insight into the process.

Albert Austin is the Northern Syndicate's administrator and the Fair Surveyor responsible for the layout of the Hoppings. In February each year an advertisement is placed in the showmen's trade journal, The World's Fair, advising of the deadline for applications for positions on the Town Moor. Many of the large rides have 'standing rights' and will appear in the same position year after year, while the positions of the sidestalls, roundstalls and juvenile rides depends on the outcome of a draw in early May. Shortly afterwards Albert and Sue Stokel-Walker, present Fair Manager, visit the Town Moor to find or replace the wooden marker pegs which identify the position of the rides. Ranging rods are used and the boundaries of the walkways, frontages and aisles are marked out using small grasscutters and white paint.

The core group of showmen who lease the Moor from the City Council and Freemen are known as the Northern Syndicate of Showmen's Guild Members. The Syndicate was formed in 1947 by founding members Jack Murphy, William Noble, Frank McConvill, Jack Hoadley and Jack Powell. Seen above in 1972, from left, are: Jack Murphy; John Murphy; and William Noble, accompanied by Fred Didsbury, Fair Manager; W. D. Nugent, assistant organiser; and Robert Cowle, ground manager.

The Northern Syndicate continues to lease the Moor and sub-let positions to the individual showfamilies. The present day members, who are all related to the founders, are Colin Noble, John Murphy (both pictured above in 2005), John Murphy Jnr, and Gertrude Powell.

Albert Austin taking final measurements from the Hoppings layout plan. When Albert was made redundant as the City's Chief Building Surveyor and Fair Manager in 1993 he became Fair Surveyor and administrator for the Northern Syndicate, continuing his involvement with the Hoppings.

Albert finding the hidden marker-pegs, four weeks before the opening of the fairground in 2004. The first peg is usually found within minutes. One year a cow chewed through Albert's tape measure. Without delays caused by pegs scattered by ploughing, the weather or hungry cows, the marking out can take up to three weeks.

The arrival of M & D's Spiderman ride in 2009. The showmen's vehicles enter the Town Moor from the Grandstand Road entrance. Pull-on day is traditionally the Sunday before the fairground's opening and all manner of vehicles can be seen arriving throughout the day. The Moor becomes a hive of activity in the early hours and is a big attraction for fair enthusiasts and the general public alike.

Joseph and Margaret Noble's 'Northern Star' lorry and living wagon on the Moor in 1952. The living wagon was built at Tyne Dock.

"It was common for visitors to the Moor to knock on the door of my parents' living wagon and ask to have a look inside. People were amazed at how beautiful it was. I remember the day the photo was taken as I drove from the Town Moor to Billingham. It was my first official drive on the roads."

Colin Noble Snr

Showman Keith Turner guides his Seddon & Atkinson lorry and packed up Imperial Waltzer into position 20 on pull-on day 2003.

Over the following days pieces of the machine are carefully unpacked and constructed.

The building up of the Waltzer on the Moor is quite leisurely over a period of days; otherwise it can be up and ready to roll within five hours.

Gradually the familiar face of the Waltzer starts to appear, as these three photographs show.

The ride started its life in 1937 as a Noah's Ark with a Ben Hur front and was owned by Will Starr.

In 1949 it was acquired by Aquilla Toogood and six years later it was rebuilt as a Waltzer with a new front featuring Bill Haley & His Comets.

Other modifications to the machine's design took place in the early 1970s before it was bought by Keith Turner in 1981 and renamed as the Imperial Waltzer.

With the ten cars in place, the finishing touches are added to the paintwork on the edge of the platforms, as seen here in 2003.

Typically there are five Waltzers on the Moor. Starting at the south end, they are Murphy's, Clark's, Turner's, Crow's and Shaw's.

The diesel set is fired up and the Waltzer is finally unveiled to the public when the fairground opens on the Friday. In 2009, the author took consecutive rides on each of the five Waltzers present on the Moor (in the interests of research). The challenge took an hour and he is not ashamed to say he needed a sit down and cold drink afterwards.

Showmen and civic guests during the official opening of the Hoppings in 2006. Flanked by the Mace bearer are: Colin Noble; Albert Noble, Chairman of the Northern Section of the Showmen's Guild; Ernest Johnson, National President of the Showmen's Guild; the Right Worshipful Mayor of Sunderland, Tom Foster; the Lord Mayor of Newcastle, Dianne Packham; and the Mayoress of Sunderland, Brenda Foster.

Following the opening ceremony it is traditional for the dignitaries and officials to tour the site. Members of the Northern Syndicate, John Murphy and Colin Noble, are accompanied aboard Mellors' Big Ben Tower ride by the Lord Mayor, Councillor Mary Carr, and guest in 2001

Civic guests on the dodgems at the Hoppings, circa 1970s.

The rivalry of two cities came head to head when the Mayor and Mayoress of Sunderland (left) collided with the Lord Mayor and Mayoress of Newcastle (right) on the dodgem cars at the Hoppings 2005.

Children hosted by the Variety Club at the Hoppings in the late 1990s. Since its origins as a Temperance Festival invited children have always been a feature of the Hoppings. Through the generosity of the showmen over a quarter of a million children with special needs have enjoyed free rides at the Hoppings since 1983.

The invited children clutching their free ride tickets at the Hoppings, circa 1996.

With the Hoppings now officially open, children and families flock to have a go on the rides and games, like this young lad on Culine's Rodeo in the 1970s.

Paul Lanagan and his daughter Adonia take a thrilling ride on a Hopper at the Hoppings in 2006. Visitor numbers can exceed a million during the fair's nine day duration.

An aerial view of the Hoppings in 2006 as seen from aboard Northumbria Police's helicopter.

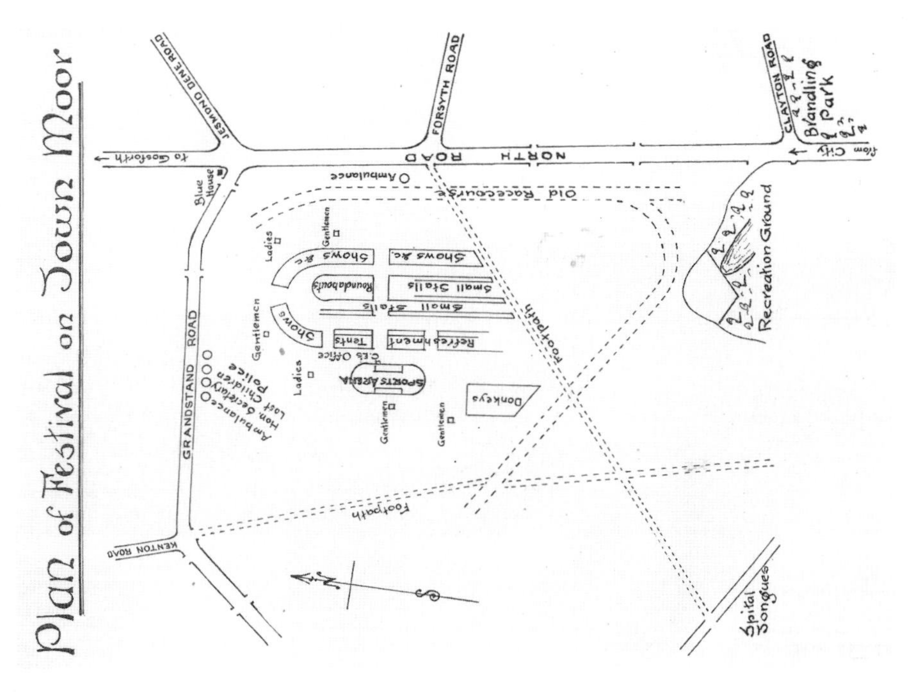

A plan of the Town Moor Fair from 1925.

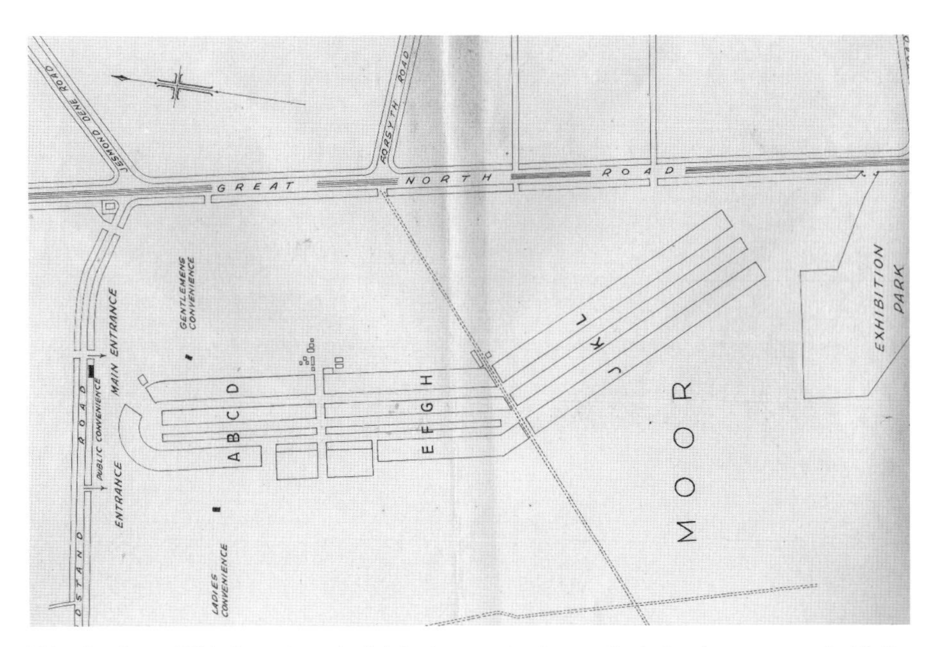

This plan from 1934 shows how the fair had grown in size, particularly when compared with the earlier plan above. The fair's position on the Moor changed as the Corporation had introduced Direct Letting to the showmen and many more machines, shows and stalls were included in the lineup.

After the lights go out on the last Saturday, the machines and stalls start to be dismantled. The sun rises in the early hours of the Sunday morning as the showmen begin to depart. The Hoppings splits up into lots of smaller town and village fairs for the rest of the year, with each particular show-family going their own separate ways. A popular misconception is that the whole fair travels away together.

Billy Crow's Foden tractor and living wagon leaving the Moor via the Forsyth path gate in 1980. Nowadays traffic exits the Moor at the northern end onto Grandstand Road.

A cow kisses John Manders' Scammell artic goodbye in 1984. The Moor is usually vacated by twelve noon on the Wednesday after the fair closes.

The Freemen now have the unenviable task of returning the Town Moor to its pre-Hoppings condition. The Moor will be cleaned, ploughed and reseeded before the cows return to graze but not before the metal detector enthusiasts have scoured the land. It is still possible to see the markings of the aisles from the air for months after the fair has departed.

HOPPINGS TIME

Who are those men, upon the Moor, that spurn the wind and rain?
They are hardy City Council lads – it's Hoppings time again!
With survey poles and measure-tapes, they're trudging up and down,
Marking out the ground, for when the Hoppings come to town.

And though it happens every year, it's still an awesome sight,
When a hundred fairground stalls and rides just mushroom overnight;
It always thrills and mystifies the curious passerby,
When a big wheel grows and blossoms in the twinkling of an eye.

To stroll around the Hoppings Fair is pleasant in the sun,
And when it rains it only brings another source of fun,
For Geordie maids in dainty shoes, beguile the lads it seems,
By skipping round the muddy pools, with girlish laughs and screams.

There are hoop-la stalls and dodgem cars, white knuckle rides as well,
Or you may prefer the music of the glittering carousel;
You can ride upon a ghost train if you're feeling rather bold,
There are gypsies that speak Geordie if you want your fortune told.

There are children's rides and shuggy boats, and hook-a-ducks abound,
There are hot dog stalls, and rocket rides that never leave the ground;
So come and see the Hoppings, sample what your fancy takes;
It's as much a part of Tyneside, as Brown Ale and stottie cakes!

Albert Austin

CHAPTER III

All the Fun of the Fair

W. H. Marshall's Mont Blanc and Big Wheel in 1949. The Mont Blanc rides first appeared in the 1930s, heralding the public's desire for faster and more thrilling rides.

An elaborate ride owned by Walter Murphy, circa 1924. This type of ride was known as a Scenic Railway, despite it having no connection to the railway whatsoever. The cars, seen behind the gentlemen, were destroyed by fire at Kenton Bank while in transit; the ride was redecorated with an oceanic theme and dolphin shaped cars.

A view of the Town Moor Fair in 1926 with Murphy's Scenic Railway in the background. The structures to the right appear to be coconut sheets (or shies).

Visitors strolling around the fairground, circa 1924. The extension chimneys, seen to the left of John Evans' large Scenic Railway, were added to the showmen's steam traction engines for the duration of the fair to ensure the smoke and smut rose above the heads of the crowd.

Green's Caterpillar ride at the Town Moor Fair, circa 1932. Underneath the canvass cover, which gave privacy to courting couples, was a ring-shaped line of cars which travelled around at speed. Sam Crow's Gallopers can be seen in the centre of the photograph.

John Murphy's Odeon Waltzer, which was built in 1947, on the Moor in 1959. The large front represented the architecture of the Odeon cinema buildings. It was removed around a year later as many of the big machines had a change of design to reflect the changing times.

A modern view of Murphy's Waltzer in 2009. The ride is well recognised around the Tyne Tees area and visits places including Houghton-le-Spring, Hartlepool, Richmond, Northallerton and Bishop Auckland.

Raymond Eddy's Energy Dome Waltzer making its fourth annual appearance at the Hoppings in 2004. Prior to this, Raymond Codona's Hell-Raiser Waltzer stood on the same position between 1983 and 2000.

Holding tight on Clark's Star Rider Disco Waltzer in 2003.

Crow's Energy Storm Waltzer, as seen on the Moor in 2004, was originally an Ark known as Easy Rider. The Ark's motorbikes were removed and replaced with rotating Waltzer cars during the conversion.

Shaw's Razzamatazz Waltzer on its usual position on the Moor, just off the Forsyth path, in 2004.

Randall William's Razzle Dazzle in 1914 when the Festival was held at Jesmond Dene. The steam powered ride, which was known as 'Whirly the Whirl', featured wooden benches arranged in a circle on a rotating and tilting platform.

Wild Thing on the Moor in 2009. This Tagada ride is a modern equivalent of the Razzle Dazzle, though the two rides are not related historically. Riders sit around the perimeter and are jostled about by the hydraulic rams underneath, providing free entertainment to the passing crowds.

Billy Whitelegg in front of his Top Spin ride in 2006. Billy is accompanied by Ernest Johnson, then President of the Showmen's Guild. The ride first appeared on the Moor in 1994, brand new from the Italian manufacturers.

Power Surge on its fourth annual visit to the Moor in 2008. The ride debuted at Sunderland Air Show in July 2003 and went on to visit Jordan in Egypt.

The Shockwave Miami Trip ride in 2009. This type of ride debuted on the British fairground scene in 1990.

One brave rider lifts her arms in the air on the Miami Trip 3 at the Hoppings in 2006. Owned by Steven Hill, the ride opened for the first time at the Swindon Link Centre in February 2005, and features impressive artwork by Paul Wright.

No visit to the Hoppings would be complete without mentioning the traditional rain and mud, as seen above in the 1970s. Walter Shaw's Moon Rockets, pictured left, last visited the Moor in 1982.

Rain and mud at the Town Moor Hoppings in 1960.

Frank Harniess's Scammell Showtrac reflected in the flooded Moor in 1963.

This family from Kenton made great use of the taps at the Forsyth Road entrance to clean the mud off their feet at the sopping Hoppings, 2007. The condition of the Moor echoed that of ten years earlier, when similar conditions occurred in 1997.

Overs' Snack Bar at the Town Moor Fair, circa 1930s. Amy Overs can be seen inside serving the gentlemen. This catering van was one of the earliest to attend the Festival.

The Overs family continues to provide food to the fairgoers of the Hoppings. Pictured above is Amy Overs' grandson, Garry Overs, in front of his food kiosk, Overeater, in 2009.

Sandra O'Brien bagging candy floss in her sweet kiosk, Munchies, next to the Forsyth Road entrance to the fair in 2006. Candy floss is an old time favourite of the fairground and is now sold in bags as health and safety rules do not permit it to be sold on wooden sticks.

World's Fair reporter, Mark McCormick, stops for a bite to eat at Thomas Morris's kiosk in 2008. Pictured behind the counter are the owner's daughters, Zarra Sheeran and Georgia Morris.

John Lock's Ghost Train standing alongside George the Gentle Giant on the show row, circa 1975. The ride was built around 1954. In the early 1980s the front was redecorated as the Spine Chilling Skeleton Express.

This 21st century ghost train, on the north-western corner of the fairground at the Hoppings in 2009, was designed, built and operated by the innovative Gilbert Chadwick Jnr.

Preparing to be shot over 180 feet into the sky on S & D Leisure's Bungee ride in 2005. Riders are secured into their seats before a nerve-wracking countdown begins and the inevitable happens. Those brave enough can relive the experience by purchasing the onboard video footage. The author was content with spectating!

Matthew & Douglas Taylor's Bomber Mark 2, possibly the fastest travelling ride in the world, at the Hoppings in 2009. Standing 55 metres tall, the arms spin around at speeds up to 80 mph. On the last Friday of the 2009 fair, a thick fog descended on the Moor and the eight riders in the top car could not be seen from the ground!

Susan Stokel-Walker, Fair Manager, with friend of the showmen, Thomas Dixon, in 1997. Thomas was minding the spotted dog for the Lord Mayor of Newcastle who was having a ride at the time of the photograph.

Playing for the big prize! Geordie lads trying their hand on Arthur Lawrence's hoopla in 2003.

The Simpson family visiting the Hoppings in 2003. The large tiger prize was as big as the children.

The Lord Mayor of Newcastle, Councillor David Slesenger, is shown how to stand the Coca-Cola bottle back up, while the Mayor of Sunderland, Councillor Bill Stephenson, and John Murphy watch in 2005.

Every little boy wants to be a train driver and this young man had his wish come true on this juvenile ride at the Hoppings in 2006.

Time for tea and a nod to the fair's Temperance Festival origins as these two girls take a whirl on a set of teacups in 2009.

CHAPTER IV

Faces from the Fairground

CHILDREN CAUGHT ON camera at the Town Moor Fair in 1938. Can any reader identify them? These were either very eager visitors or children of the showmen, perhaps out playing on a Sunday when the fair was closed.

Breakfast time on the Moor in the 1930s, a chance for the whole family to relax before the fair opens.

Local businessman and honorary member of the Showmen's Guild, Arthur J. Fenwick, chats to his showground friends (from left) Maudie Manders, Phoebe Johnson, Laura Shufflebottom, Charlotte Gregory and Stanley Crow, circa 1950. Arthur Fenwick had an interest in fairgrounds and circuses and his insightful collections of memorabilia, diaries, articles and photographs can be found in Tyne & Wear Archives.

A group of showmen taking time out from the fair, circa 1908. The first three of the sitting gentlemen, from left, are: Richard Monte; Jim Monte; and Johnny Murphy. Johnny was one of the first showmen to present rides at the Temperance Festival in the 1880s. His son, Jack Murphy, can be seen on page 14, while his grandson and great-grandson, both called John, can be seen on the next page.

Walter Murphy's Burrell traction engine in 1925. This engine was used to transport the loads carrying his huge Scenic Railway (as seen on page 30).

Murphy's Waltzer on the Town Moor in 2007. On the dancer are John Murphy and his grandson, Rory Freeman. John's daughter, Alison, can be seen sitting in the pay box.

John Murphy Jnr in the pay box of his Dodgems, 2007. John is the fifth of six generations of the Murphy family to present rides at the Hoppings.

Paul Stevens with his set of Shuggy Boats in 2008 – probably the oldest ride on the Moor.

"The Shuggy Boats were built in 1896 by my Granddad, John Henry Stevens, at a cost of £28, which was a fortune then. They have been in the family since and are a family heirloom; I wouldn't part with them. They take two hours to build up and I could do it with my eyes shut now. I get a lot of comments and feedback from the public, particularly the grannies, who can remember going on them when they were younger. Peter Beardsley's been on them a few times and I never take any money from him. If Alan Shearer came along, I'd lift him on for free!"

Paul Stevens

Three generations from the Noble family at the Hoppings, circa 2001. Pictured are, from left: Darren Noble, Colin Noble Jnr, Darren Noble Jnr, and Colin Noble.

Lesley Noble in the pay box of Noble's Dodgems, 2007.

Gilbert Chadwick Snr outside his Fun House in 2003.

Billy Freeman with his Rotor in 2008. This type of ride first appeared on the Moor in 1951 and was known to the public as the 'sticky wall'.

Showman Arthur Lawrence in his Hoopla sidestall at the Hoppings in 2003.

Jo Dean in her contemporary version of Hook-a-Duck, 2003. The first Hook-a-Duck appeared on the Moor in 1958.

Fair enthusiast Thomas Dixon takes a ride on Crow's gallopers at the Hoppings in 2005. Thomas has been visiting the Town Moor Fair since 1934 and has only missed the civic opening twice since 1947.

'Ginger Johnny' (John Brown) beside the Rolling Thunder Waltzer in 2003. The special certificate was to mark the fortieth anniversary of his time with the machine. He jokingly says that Aquilla Toogood sold him with the ride when it passed to Keith Turner in the 1980s.

John Culine in the centre of his Silver Rodeo, circa 1970s. At the time, his Rodeo was the only platform ride on the Moor to go both forwards and backwards, which often gave riders a fright! One year, when the horses were touched up with paint, John could be seen sporting shoes with silver soles!

Lisa Newsome and her son, Arthur, at a very muddy Hoppings in 2007. Wellington boots were definitely in vogue this year.

John Gale, fourth from left, and his friends at the Town Moor Festival in June 1955. John Gale's fairground photograph collection is housed at the National Fairground Archive and offers a unique record of the North East's fairground heritage.

Fair enthusiasts waiting for the Hoppings' official opening to get underway in 2006. The enthusiasts collect photographs and videos of the fairground and attend model shows all over the country. Their interests can cover the traditional rides, the artwork, the big hitters and even the transport side of the business.

Valerie Moody M.B.E., an Education Liaison Officer for the Showmen's Guild, and her train ride in 2003. As with the other juvenile rides, this particular one moves around the Moor each year depending on the result of a ballot.

"The Town Moor has always been special to me and my family. My earliest recollection of the Town Moor as a youngster is a one of excitement; I would put the clock forward two hours so we could get there on time! The Town Moor has a magic of its own and it's a wonderful fair with special memories – I met my husband there. I've been the Northern Section's Education Liaison Officer for over twenty-one years and the National Education Officer for around 12 years. Together with Maureen Bowman, a traveller teacher, we went round the showmen with children, trailer to trailer, and had an exhaustive time on the Moor. Maureen spoke to the fairground manager, Albert Austin, and he said we could use the cabins at the fairground entrance. The Town Moor Fair School was founded and the parents, the showmen from all around the country who bring their children, now regard the school as part of the Town Moor. The school has visits from educationalists from all around the country and I work as host, doing the PR work for the school. The school is a source of privilege and pride, a chance for the showmen's children to network and meet their friends of the future."

Valerie Moody M.B.E.

Allan Jones in his traditional coconut sheet, 2005. The sidestall, which was originally his grandfather's, is one of the oldest attractions on the Town Moor today and dates from around 1917.

Walter Murphy with his juvenile ride on the Moor in 2003.

Maureen Austin, wife of Fair Surveyor Albert Austin, in the police mess cabin at Hoppings Control in 2004.

"I became associated with the Hoppings in 1988 when my husband Albert became Chief Building Surveyor for Newcastle City Council. Once the showmen began to arrive I would sit in Albert's office to take any messages or give out any telephone numbers that were asked for while Albert was attending to anything that needed to be done. All of the things I do are voluntary. My first role was an emergency situation – to order and serve the number of required meals for the police – that was quite stressful. I now look after the showmen's mail as the Hoppings has its own postcode (NE2 3DA), prepare the cabins at Hoppings Control for use by the Fair School in the morning, keep the tea urn filled and make drinks for the police. I occasionally look after lost children when the attendant is not there after 10pm; however the number has dropped over the years. You get a good tan on the Moor and all my friends ask me where I have been."

Maureen Austin

Millie Barrass minding the cups in 2004. Millie is a friend of the Turner family and helps out at the Moor – on her week's holiday from her regular job.

The Lord Mayor of Newcastle, Councillor John Marshall (left), exchanges gifts with John Houghton, then President of the Showmen's Guild, at the annual cocktail reception in the Civic Centre, 2002. This is traditionally held early in the evening on the first day of the Hoppings and is jointly hosted by the showmen and the City.

The Lord Mayor of Newcastle on his official tour of the fairground in 2008. Pictured are, from left: Phillip Cooper Jnr; the Lord Mayor, Councillor David Wood; Phillip Cooper Snr; and John Murphy. The juvenile ride behind the gentlemen was in its 66th year on the Moor having been built by Phillip Snr's father, Les, in 1942. The author enjoyed this ride as a child on its visits to Houghton Feast.

Alan A. Cowie with his toy set model ride at the Hoppings in 2003. Alan has had the ride, which was made by Hawtins of Blackpool, for over forty years.

Lana Turner in the pay box of Licence to Thrill, 2006.

"I have been attending the Moor since I was 11 months old. I used to stand in the Waltzer pay box with my Dad and give the change out to the men who helped us. My Mam tells me that when I was a baby I used to sit in my Silver Cross pram, watching my Dad and brothers build up. It is traditional for the showmen's children to attend the annual kids' dance while on the Moor. My Mam used to put me in frilly dresses, also a showmen tradition I'm sure, until I was old enough to decide that I wanted to wear denim jeans and a cropped vest! I loved the dances, which were held at the Moat House Hotel at the Silverlink. All the kids used to come out and go over the road to McDonalds, put the straws in the paper that they came in, and blow them at each other. Then it moved to South Shields and that's where I spent my last dance when I was 12. I still remember it as if it was yesterday; all our crew singing Run DMC and trying to copy the dances out of the video in the middle of the dance floor! As I got older, from 14, I started minding the Sea Storm ride, and I think that's where memories were made because that's what I still hear today from the other traveller boys and girls, about how they used to come up and have a little chat to me on my boats. I was promoted to the Teacups, then, when I was 20, the Frogs. There is no better feeling in the world than a showman minding their machine at Newcastle Town Moor, especially if you're busy; there is so much competition that you know you have got to be doing something right!"

Lana Turner

Brian O'Brien with his cup 'n' saucer juvenile ride in 2003. Brian has been visiting the Town Moor all of his life, having been born there in 1938.

Claire O'Brien on a kiddies' toy set in 2006. Note the website address on the back of the car. Many show-families have their own websites, a sign of the times. The World's Fair and telegrams were originally used but mobile phones and email have revolutionised communication between showmen.

Darren Noble, Colin Noble Jnr, Keith Turner and his sons Keith and Brett at the Hoppings, circa 1996.

"I first visited the Hoppings in June 1949, as I was born in July 1948. My father, who was born in Gateshead in 1917, and his father visited before me. When we purchased our Waltzer in 1981 we signed the contracts on the first Friday of the Hoppings, but we did not take full control until the Saturday. The reason being because showmen are superstitious - if you buy something new you do not open it on a Friday. Therefore we left the Friday's income with Aquilla Toogood. I was the Chairman of the Northern Section of the Showmen's Guild in 1989 – the year of the Guild's centenary. A documentary was made about me and my family that year, called 'After the Lights Go Out' by Jeff Brown. I remember an incident in 1962. There was an agricultural show on at the back of the Hoppings and a dome shaped container blew over the caravans. Other memorable times were the rain and the mud, the dances and socialising with people you very rarely saw."

Keith Turner

Colin the Lampman in his mobile electrical outlet on Swag Man's Alley, a trade section of the Hoppings for the showmen, 2005. Colin sells a wide range of accessories for the fairground, including bulbs, bolts, and disco lights. He has been attending the Hoppings for over thirty years and was first introduced to the Town Moor and Hull Fair by his best friend, the late showman Andrew Bell.

John Wilkins at his swag unit on Swag Man's Alley in 2005. John has been supplying the showmen with their prizes for over 40 years. In 1931 a trade section was first introduced to the Temperance Festival and sold such things as meat, bread and groceries.

Ann Shaw, a toy seller, at her stall on the Moor in 2004. Ann has been selling toy dolls since 1954 and finds that they are still popular today.

Steve Barratts and his eye catching bowler hat bring smiling customers to Tommy Cole's coconut stand in 2004.

The Mayor of Sunderland, Juliana Heron, and the Lady Mayoress, Marie Adamson, taking a ride on the gallopers at the Hoppings 2003. Traditionally the Mayor of Sunderland is always invited to the fairground as a guest of the Lord Mayor of Newcastle.

Leonard Fenwick, Chairman of the Steward's Committee of Freemen, making a speech at the official opening of the Hoppings in 2005. In 2008 Mr Fenwick was knighted in the Queen's Birthday Honours List.

Showmen, Freemen and Civic guests gather with the Lord Mayor for the customary photograph after the opening of the Hoppings in 2008.

The Lord Mayor of Newcastle's Mace and Sword bearers, Trevor Cartner and Malcolm Osbourn, at the Hoppings in 2005. The Great Mace dates from 1687.

Sue Stokel-Walker, Fair Manager, at the north end of the fairground in 2003.

Peter Scott, a Recreational Development Officer at Newcastle Council, pastes up a notice for the Lost Children cabin, 2009.

David Jones from 'David Jones' Locker' in 2004. David started selling cockles, mussels and prawns on the Moor in 1989, and is well known for visiting the local bars and clubs.

Jeff Brown, a former producer of Channel 4's groundbreaking music show 'The Tube', on the Moor in 2004. Jeff became involved with fairgrounds at an early age when he used to buy the vinyl records for use on 'Uncle Quilly' Toogood's Waltzer. He went on to direct 'After the Lights Go Out', a behind the scenes documentary into the life of a showman's family, and also 'The Story of the Hoppings'.

Mark McCormick from World's Fair next to a set of small gallopers in 2004.

"My interest in fairgrounds started at a very early age as my Dad regularly took the family to fairs in the region. The main ones I remember were Shiremoor Children's Treat, and the Spanish City at Whitley Bay, as well as Ocean Beach Pleasure Park at South Shields, but he always found a reason for the pair of us to return to the Hoppings. I first heard of World's Fair newspaper back in 1995 when I would regularly read up on the Moor and other fairs in the archive section of Newcastle Central Library. I started taking it back home in May 1996 and I did my first sample report on Blyth Christmas Fair two years later. I now write frequently for World's Fair; I compile my report on all the major attractions in attendance, using my judgement, knowledge and memories as to which attractions are worthy of a special mention. I can often be seen during the Hoppings talking to the many showmen I have come to know."

Mark McCormick

CHAPTER V

The Sideshows

The famous show row at the Hoppings in 1955.

THERE HAS ALWAYS been a wide range of entertainment on the Moor beyond the thrill of a ride on a roundabout. Right from the earliest Festivals the showmen have been erecting their booths and presenting shows and exhibitions, offering the visiting public rare chances to see exotic wild animals, waxwork models, marionette shows, mysterious moving pictures in the days before the cinema, thrilling motorcycle stunts, pugilistic heroes, and even oddities and freaks from around the country. Times and tastes have changed and the Hoppings now has more rides than shows. The photographs in this chapter contain a selection of some of these alternative forms of amusement which were mostly found along the famous show row at the northwest end of the fairground.

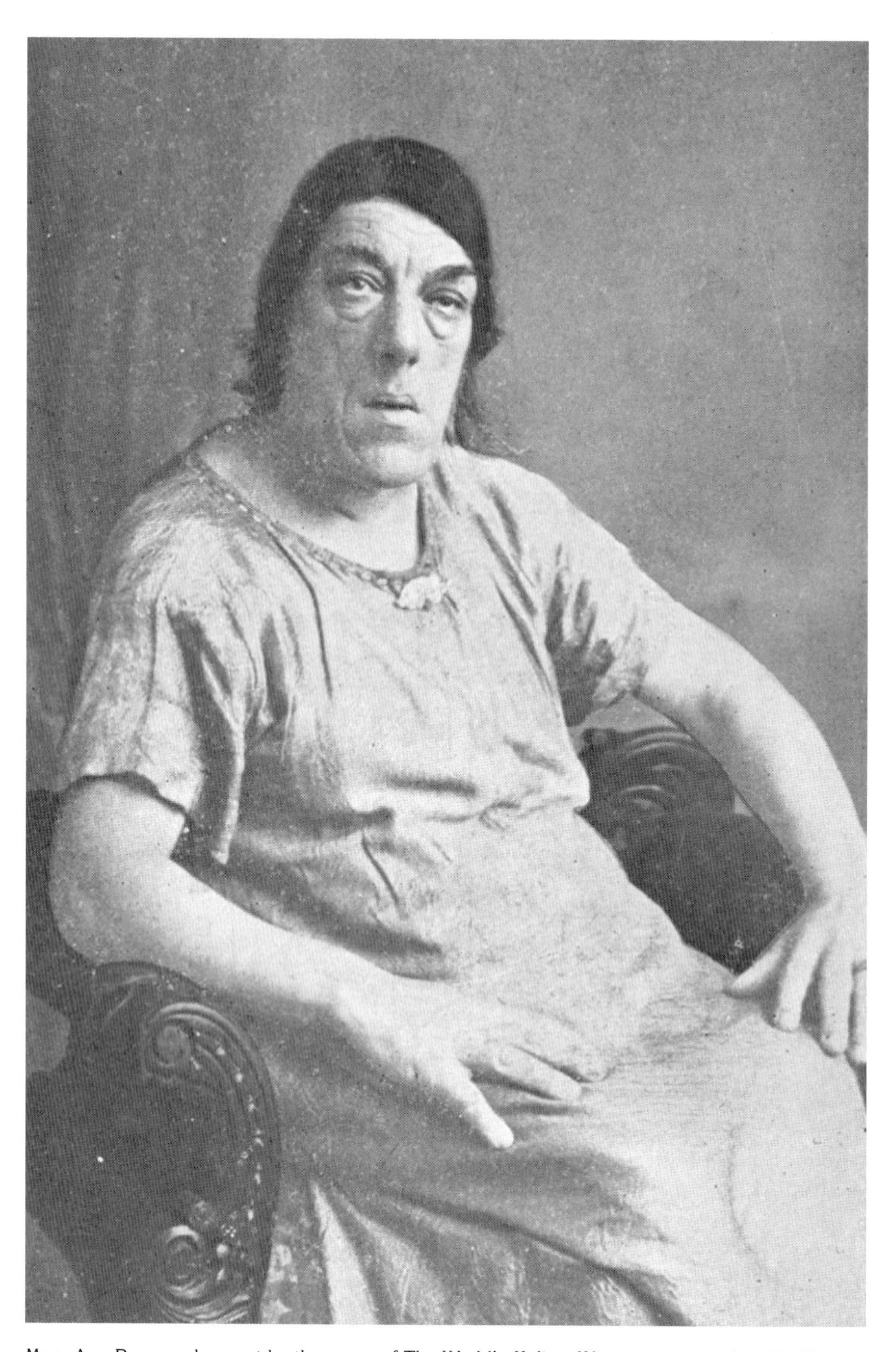

Mary Ann Bevan, who went by the name of The World's Ugliest Woman, appeared on the Moor in the 1930s having previously appeared in Barnum & Bailey's American circus. Mary Ann's physical abnormalities apparently developed after the sudden death of her husband in 1914 and she became involved with a sideshow after winning an ugly woman contest. The World's Fair reported her death on December 26th 1933 at the age of 59.

Robert Hill's 'Believe It Or Not' collection of oddities from around the world is a regular attraction on the show row at the Hoppings. It was owned by Robert's late father, William Hill, and was originally known as the Museum of Oddities.

This unique collection features a giant rat as big as a dog; the Indian elephant boy who has a trunk for a nose; the extraordinary Capella, the two headed giant; the Japanese octopus; vampire bats from Transylvania; the nutty two tail squirrel; the shrunken head from New Guinea; the American kitten with two bodies, eight legs and one head; the Siamese twin monkeys from the Amazon; a memento of the Berlin Wall; the two headed stoat; the smallest horse in the world; the German pig with six legs; and Mr Big Mouth from Hull.

A crowd gathers in front of Ron Taylor's Wrestling & Boxing Booth, the Excelsior Pavilion, ahead of the big fight in 1963. The winner was guaranteed five pounds, while the loser would get a 'bloody good hiding'.

A view of Ron Taylor's boxing and wrestling booth in the 1980s. This frontage was painted by fairground artist Paul Wright following the booth's involvement in a road accident in 1979. The flash features Ron's face, top left, and Muhammad Ali, top right, who had sparred at the booth on a visit to South Shields in July 1977.

Ron Taylor, seen above in 2003, would often comment in the local press about the abundance of contenders in Newcastle. He first brought the booth to the Moor in 1951 but had been travelling with it since 1936 following his father's death. At one time there were more than fifty travelling boxing booths in the country (three attended the Town Moor Fair of 1929), but Ron's was the last still in business. He was a regular visitor to the Hoppings, even after the booth's last visit in 1995. Ron passed away on July 20th 2006 at the age of ninety-five.

The Masked with Rob Roy MacGregor, circa 1972. The wrestlers would stand on the show front to attract the people into the show. Rob Roy was Scottish champion for around fifteen years. The masked wrestler, who sometimes went by the name of The Panda, was a businessman from Newcastle.

Ringside views of Taylor's boxing and wrestling booth, circa 1978, with Richard Lanagan as referee.

"I first wrestled in Ron Taylor's booth in 1966. I was taught by a well-known wrestler called Charles Henry, and by Peter Macklin who is now retired in Australia. I wrestled for 20 years and used the name 'Shamus Lanagan'. Once, a man challenged anybody to fight and out of the crowd stepped Pat Roach – the man ran away and never came back. Another lad wanted to fight 'The Masked'; he received a broken nose and cracked ribs and, again, never came back. Other wrestlers who were at the booth between 1966 and 1986 included: Boy Devlin; The Farmer's Boy (Peter Hornsby); Ken Davis; Dynamite Dickie Swales; Arnie Bullier (Durham Ox); Ken Prest; The Mighty Joe Robinson; Neil Kincaid; the Rev Michael Brooks; Frankie Robb; Robbie Earl; Dave Webb; Bob Barron; and Norman Cooper. Some of the boxers at this time were: Danny Warty; Steve Wilson; Eddie Morton; Peter Oxman; and The Lumberjack."

Richard Lanagan

George Gracie, the Gentle Giant, was Scotland's tallest living man at 7ft 3 inches. He had a 56 inch chest and waist, a 21 inch collar and wore size 18 shoes.

He made many visits to the Town Moor in the 1970s and 1980s.

Children aboard the Buzz Bombs ride in 1950, with a glimpse of the shows behind. The three shows to the right are: Omi the Man Made Monster; Satan's Daughter; and the Tattooed Lady. The Great Omi's real name was Horace Ridley, a man from London, who made his living as a sideshow act from his stripy black tattoos. He also went by the name of the Zebra Man.

The fronts of three sideshows at the Hoppings in the 1970s. Seen here are: King Kong Alive; The Great Unknown (Freaks of Nature); and everyone's favourite, the Magic Mirrors. Can any reader remember what lay behind these doorways?

Fairgoers gather around Joseph Noble's brand new Housey Housey in 1954. Colin Noble can be seen at the microphone calling out the numbers. Costing sixpence a ticket, players stood a chance of winning a range of prizes from those on offer, such as: household goods, big toys, prize dolls, footballs and tennis rackets. The word 'bingo', influenced by the American game, didn't become popular until much later, at around the same time as when seating was introduced to the perimeter of the roundstalls.

Another of the Nobles' Housey Housey stalls at the Town Moor Fair, circa 1948. At this time, there were over sixty ticket joints at the fair and they were considered to be the 'capital of entertainment' on the Moor.

Don't be shy, give it a try! George Robert Hanley calls the numbers in his Las Vegas Prize Bingo in 2006. George Robert has been visiting the Moor for over twenty-five years.

A night at the fair with a stash of prizes from Charlie Goodall's Spinner in 1952. Pictured are, from left: Martin Clews; Stella Clews, with the doll; Pat Cross; and George Cross on the miniature galloping horse.

Eyes down with the Lord Mayor, Councillor Belle Nixon (second lady from the left), on Edward Bliss's Famous Prize Bingo, 1997.

Elizabeth Bensley and her son Edward playing for a full house on Peter Richardson's Housey Housey stall, 2008

Messham's Wall of Death, the World Famous Motor Cycle Stunt Show, made a welcome appearance at the Hoppings in 2008 having opened in August 2007. Several Walls of Death have appeared at the Moor over the years, including Albert Evans' 20th Century Stunt Show in the 1950s, where patrons could see Albert performing as 'Cyclone Al'.

James Messham doing 'no hands' at the front of the show, a hint at some of the spectacular stunts you could see inside.

Members of the Messham family chat with the dignitaries following the official opening of the Hoppings in 2008. The Messham family have had a Wall of Death since the 1930s.

Hoppings organisers John Murphy (left) and Colin Noble (right) pose with James Messham and his sons, Jake and Junior, outside of the Wall of Death.

Civic guests, dignitaries and members of the Showmen's Guild look down from the gallery into the drum shaped arena. The show is about to begin!

The stars of the show welcome the special guests to the Wall of Death. The bikes used in the show are Honda XRs (125) and Indian Scouts from the 1920s.

The Wall of Death soon fills with the roar of the engines, the smell of petrol and the audience's applause and gasps as the bikes come perilously close to the top (see page 5). It is customary for the audience to throw down coins at the end of the show as a mark of appreciation for the death-defying stunts.

A baby elephant visited the Moor with Bostock & Wombwell's Menagerie in 1912. This portable zoo was founded by George Wombwell in the late 1800s and travelled all around the country with an exotic range of animals until its last performance (coincidentally) in Newcastle in 1931.

Crowds approaching the frontage of Pinder's Big Zoo Circus Show in 1938 while the barker calls out about the new programme and guarantee of a seat. For the entrance fee of 6d (2 ½ p in today's coinage) you could see a wide collection of circus acts and animals, including performing lions.

Lyndsay Frain riding on a donkey in the 1980s. Donkey rides have long been a feature at the Hoppings; the outline of a donkey enclosure is clearly marked out on the Festival layout plan of 1925.

Mr Smith and Tyson the Donkey in 2006.

Another popular attraction at the Hoppings are the palmists and fortune tellers. Seen here are Rene Allison and her daughter Vira in the late 1930s. At that time the palmists' caravans were in a different position on the Moor to that of today.

Ronica Allison and Dilly Allison with their niece, Vira Allison (centre), at the lower end of the Town Moor in the late 1940s.

Vira Allison and her two granddaughters, Cheyenne and Denver, in 2006. The caravan still occupies the same position as that in the photograph above. Vira, who was born in Kendal, has been coming to the Moor all of her life, her family having visited previously. She now regards her annual visit to the Moor as 'traditional'.

The lines of traditional and contemporary gypsy caravans extend down the south end of the Town Moor towards the Exhibition Park entrance. The information boards are works of art in their own right, and make fascinating reading. A selection of them is seen here in 2006.

Kathleen Lee, Queen of the Gypsies, inside her traditional caravan on the Town Moor in 2007. Many of the palm readers are of the Romany ethnic group and are not to be confused with the travelling showmen.

Sarah Sherwood in her caravan in 2003.

"It is a gift; my mother, aunts and sisters all do the same. I use tarot cards and do palm readings. One hand is a character reading, but two hands read together is a full reading, showing past, present and future. I hope for good weather and for people to come to enjoy themselves at the Hoppings."

Sarah Sherwood

Kookie Smith crystal gazing in her caravan, 2007.

Michele Wheatley minding the Outer Limits in 2003. Now owned by John Wheatley, this fun house is a familiar face on the show row and has been appearing since it was built by his father, Fred, in 1965.

Beverly Manders outside of the Glass House on the Moor in 2003. The perplexing maze originated in the USA and takes only fifty minutes to build up.

Gilbert Chadwick Jnr first brought his Maze of Terror to the Moor in 2005. The walk-through experience was designed and built by Gilbert himself and offered those brave enough to enter a guaranteed fright on the show row! It has visited the Hoppings every year since and is now owned by Jimmy Stokes. The Chadwick family has always had a strong presence on the show row, with Gilbert's father, Gilbert Snr, presenting a freak show for many years, followed by a two storey Fun House.

Barry the King of Guessers on a very muddy Moor in 2007. Barry, who is typically located at the southern end of the site, will guess your age within one year – or you win a prize. He has been doing the challenge since he was nine years old. A similar novelty appeared on the Moor in 1950 - Lee Bennett of Montreal, who was dressed as a cowboy!

The Queen of the Nile sideshow in 1980. The sign to the left reads: "Not recommended for those with a weak or nervous disposition". The show was presented by Michael Mason, who even had a mouse circus, featuring one hundred performing mice in a miniature fairground.

Keith Carroll's 'Strange Girls' on the Moor in 1980. The show featured photographs of babies with three legs, midgets, and hairy women, amongst others. Admission was 60p.

CHAPTER VI

The Town Moor Fair School

MANY VISITORS TO the modern day Hoppings fairground are often surprised to see the 'Town Moor Fair School' sign when they enter the Moor at the Forsyth Road gate. But the sign is correctly placed, as the Hoppings HQ cabins are used as classrooms for the travelling children during the day, before doubling up as mess rooms for the police and St John Ambulance while the fair is in operation. The school was founded in 1988 by Maureen Bowman, a traveller support teacher. The temporary school is open for the duration of the fair and is now organised by Newcastle Ethnic Minority, Traveller and Refugee Achievement Service. Thirty-four children attended in the first year; nowadays around eighty children are on roll.

Although not connected to the present school, a well-known face on the Town Moor in the 1930s and 1940s was that of Mrs Sarah Brown, a widow of a Methodist minister, who would come along to teach the children. 'Auntie Brown', as she was known to the children, had converted a bus into a classroom with desks and an organ inside. She would follow the local fairs and give the children the opportunity of an education. One member of the show community, Pat Smith, recollects marching around the Town Moor with Auntie Brown leading the way singing the hymn, 'Onward, Christian Soldiers'.

"During his tour of the Newcastle Race Week Fair, Mr T. E. Browne, the Vice-President of the Showmen's Guild, paid a visit to Auntie Brown's school for showmen's children. Addressing the scholars, Mr Browne suggested that they might have a half-holiday in honour of his visit, but on being asked if they wanted a holiday they one and all shouted "No!" However, cheers soon broke out when the Vice-President promised to send them all some chocolate."

World's Fair, June 26th 1937

Each year the Town Moor Fair School goes from strength to strength and here Maureen Bowman, seen above in 1989 when a police horse visited the school, recollects the early years of the school:

"In the mid 1980s, many of the winter base schools for the children of showmen were being encouraged to prepare work packs for their pupils to take when travelling with the various fairs. It was agreed that the support teachers throughout the country would try to visit these fairs and assist children with the school-prepared work pack so that the child would be less likely to fall behind. So in June 1988 I approached Albert Austin, who at that time was Chief Building Surveyor and responsible for overseeing the set up of the fair, to ask where I would find the two or three children who I knew would be at the Hoppings that year. It was Albert who suggested that the children should come to me rather than me seek them out in their various trailers. And so the school began. Maureen Austin, Albert's wife, borrowed chairs and tables from her local church and set up the police refreshment room as a classroom.

I had had a small allowance as a support teacher, which had been used to equip a classroom in the west end of Newcastle; this I stripped bare, and with all I could collect or borrow, I moved into the police headquarters. That first year was very trial and error. I was not even sure I had permission to be there from the Authority so when newspapers, radio and TV arrived, I did a disappearing act!

Maureen Bowman with children at the school in 1994. The new hardstanding floor allowed more activities to take place outside of the cabins.

The whole venture was only made possible by the support teachers from Gateshead, Durham, Middlesbrough, North Tyneside and Sunderland, all coming to support children from their authority and bringing materials which were eagerly received.

From the beginning Maureen Austin was pivotal in making it happen. Not only did she provide the tables and chairs but she worked with groups of children, listening to them read, painting, gluing and sticking, and playing board games, but most important to me, she washed the brushes and tables, swept and mopped the floors, made the coffee and provided the biscuits and home made fruit cake; she was a constant support for everything I tried to achieve.

Another more than useful pair of hands was Alasdair MacKenzie, an Education Welfare Officer from Newcastle, who helped with attendance. I don't know how he did it, and I never dared to ask, but he managed to find time to be at the school most days. He did all the usual tasks of helping with work packs, reading, and craft work, but he also helped with the transportation of all the things I eventually managed to beg, borrow or acquire.

That first year we had thirty-four children visit the school, varying from three years old to thirteen, most of whom came every day. In subsequent years, children had to be of school age but parents of younger children could use the sand and water activities with their children.

Freda Miller, a long-term volunteer, seen at the Fair School in 1996.

The school packs were still in their infancy and only one or two children had any work from their school, so it was instant on the spot assessment with hundreds of worksheets I had amassed as a special needs support teacher in previous years. This was actually more successful than it sounds, as children are well able to select work which they can do and teachers very quickly spot when that work is not challenging enough. The children were expected to do some mathematics, written or language work and reading to an adult – here is where I used all my retired teacher friends, students and Freda Miller, wife of one of the Freemen, who came regularly over the years to help me. The rest of the day was spent creatively, painting, pottery, sand and water play, models and board games, with cards being an especially favourite pastime for the boys.

However the day was short. During the second week of the school, the fair would start early in the afternoon and the police would begin to arrive soon after one o'clock. That first year we had to pretend we did not exist but as the years went by we took over more and more cabins, decorated them with our pictures and photographs and even stopped hiding things away. In fact it soon became evident that the police were using our classroom not as it was originally or officially set up.

As the work packs improved and children were being supported more in other fairgrounds around the country, my aim was to provide more social activities, where the children could share in a project which would be more difficult to do in isolation in their trailer. Creative works became more organised. We built giant models, made musical instruments, and designed spacecraft, although they still had to do about an hour on their work pack first.

Party time at the Fair School in 1996. The last day is always a bitter-sweet occasion.

As the school grew year on year, it had to be split into a class of children aged under seven and a class of over seven, which sometimes caused problems, as siblings did not want to be separated. Gradually over the years a set of unwritten rules evolved. Children under seven who were brought to the school by parents or older children had to leave the name of the person who would collect them. Some days I was given as many as four names for 'collectors' but as long as their names were on the list it was okay.

On the last day of school we always had a party, with music, dancing, singing and party games, followed by drinks and snacks and sad goodbyes for another year.

Some years, as many as eighty children would visit the school with as many as thirty at any one time. One year we were asked to help someone with her French, and we did, another year it was research for a history project. On one occasion a parent wanted advice on reading books and I later got a letter saying how pleased she was and how successful the books had been; a few years ago I went back to visit the school and a young man who I had known since he was three came to see me. William Wassell had grown into such a fine young man that it made me proud to feel that I may have had some small influence in his education."

Maureen Bowman

Children at the Town Moor Fair School in 1998, with Maureen Austin in the background. The children work through packs provided by their winter base schools for the first part of the session, followed by practical based activities after break time. Nowadays the children can keep in touch with their winter base schools through email on laptop computers with remote Internet access.

Some of the younger children from the Town Moor Fair School playing outdoors with the sand and water, circa 1992. A young William Wassell can be seen approaching the sandpit.

"Maureen Bowman was an inspiration for me. My very first day at the Town Moor Fair School sticks out. Unused to being at school, and very unimpressed with not being able to simply play all day, I managed to escape, only to be given chase by Maureen. Being only small I evaded her by crawling underneath a lorry and then squeezing through a dolly lock, very pleased with myself. Poor old Maureen had to run the long way round, and was somewhat out of breath when she arrived at our wagon five minutes later to cart me back. We laugh about that even now. I must say, after I'd given it a chance, I did enjoy the school, and it was a big help towards my education."

William Wassell

The showmen's children on a tour of the fairground in 2004. The children took great delight in pointing out which rides 'they' owned.

Maureen Austin presents Diane Barlow with a bouquet of flowers on behalf of the Town Moor Fair School upon Diane's retirement in 2005. Diane, one of the school's organisers, first became involved in 1999 when she attended as a part-time traveller teacher.

An arty-clarty activity in one of the school's cabin classrooms in 2005. Pictured is traveller teacher Kath Wilson from Middlesbrough Traveller Education Consortium. The children made magic folding wallets which made paper money disappear.

Traveller teacher Diana Neville-Smith, left, and volunteer Ruth Lewis working with the children on a craft activity of paper weaving in 2007.

BBC radio Newcastle presenter, Ian Robinson, lets the children say hello live on air when the BBC Blue Bus came to the Hoppings in 2005. The children climbed onboard and were able to utilise the computer facilities on the bus.

Lewis Stokes watches with the showmen's children at the screening of their homemade documentary DVD in 2007. The activity was organised by the Traveller Youth Project.

Sarah Edgar fielding during the Fair School's first annual game of Rounders in 2005. Sarah, a traveller teacher from Newcastle Ethnic Minority, Traveller & Refugee Achievement Service, became teacher in charge of the school in 2006 following the retirement of Diane Barlow.

Darren Noble going in for a strike at the Fair School's annual game of Rounders in 2006. How many children go to school with the backdrop of one of the largest fairgrounds in the World?

Teacher Bob Day reads a story to the children at the school in 2004.

Katie Gascoigne and Paul Lanagan, volunteers at the Fair School, look on during a playtime in 2005.

Paul Lanagan with Year 1/2 on the last day of school in 2007. The children had a Harry Potter craft day and made wizard hats and flags as a special treat.

Pupils pose in front of the fossilized Tyrannosaurus Rex at the Great North Museum in 2009. The opening of the new museum and its proximity to the Town Moor provided an ideal opportunity for a school trip.

Valerie Moody M.B.E., National Education Liaison Officer for the Showmen's Guild, gives out certificates of achievement on the last day of school in 2006.

The school played host to Civic Guests when the Lord Mayor of Newcastle arrived to give out certificates of achievement to the pupils of the Fair School in 2009. Pictured here, from left, are: Dorrie Cookson, Lady Mayoress; Albert Austin; Councillor Michael Cookson, the Lord Mayor; and two pupils from the school.

CHAPTER VII

Hoppings Time Line

Making final preparations for the opening of the Temperance Festival in the 1890s. Programmes were a penny each (see page 8).

NO TWO YEARS at the Hoppings are ever the same, be that the line up, the crowds, the atmosphere, or even the weather, and this is reflected in the following Time Line, which covers the fairground's heritage throughout the three eras – its origins in 1882 as a Temperance Festival, promoting abstinence and the evils of alcohol; the transitional phase of Town Moor Fair, with shows and entertainment; and since the 1950s, as the Hoppings, a huge fairground, with modern rides to suit all tastes.

One consistency throughout the history of the Hoppings has been the involvement of the Murphy family. In the 1880s and early 1900s, amusements were provided by three brothers, Johnny, William and Walter Murphy: William was recorded as being lessee of the Moor in 1887, and Johnny in 1899. Over a hundred years later, to the present, and the Murphys are still involved with the organisation of the fairground: Johnny's son, Jack, was a founding member of the Northern Syndicate in 1947, while his grandson and great-grandson, both called John, are current members of the Syndicate. Johnny's great-great grandchildren, John Henry Murphy, Rory Freeman and Spencer Freeman continue to be involved with the fairground.

Customers patronising an iced lemon drinks stand at the Temperance Festival, circa 1898. Costing a halfpenny per glass, what could be better for a hot day on the Moor?

1721 - The annual Northumberland horseracing meeting relocated to Newcastle's Town Moor from Killingworth.

1771 - A dispute arose between the Freemen and town magistrates over the ownership of the Moor. Ownership was vested in the Corporation of the City of Newcastle upon Tyne, however grazing rights were granted to the Freemen.

1823 – The well-known clown, Billy Purvis, set up his booth on the Town Moor at the Newcastle Races; during a tirade with a fellow showman, he used the word 'Geordie'. Billy died in 1853 and never made it to the actual Town Moor Fair.

1881 - The Gosforth Park Racing Company took control of the races from the Grand Stand Company (a public body).

1882 - A dispute between the Corporation and the Gosforth Park Racing Company resulted in the races moving from the Town Moor to Gosforth. The North of England Temperance Festival Association held a festival on the Town Moor as a counter attraction during Race Week. 150,000 people attended the two day event and no cases of drunkenness were reported. Mr R. F. W. Liddle was Temperance Festival manager. Rent paid by the showmen is thought to have been £10.

"A Temperance Festival was held the same day on the Town Moor, Newcastle-on-Tyne, where the races have been held for nearly 150 years. The removal of the races to Gosforth Park, where the admission fee was a shilling, leads to the counter attraction in the way of public amusements. A band contest, football, cricket, foot-racing, and other sports were organised, for which good prizes were given, and addresses were delivered. The people present were estimated at 150,000. No intoxicating drinks were allowed to be sold."

Illustrated London News, July 8th 1882

Contrasting clothes at the Temperance Festival in the 1890s. The cowboy style hats and boots suggest that these gentlemen were from outside of the Newcastle area.

1883 – The organisers planned to make the Festival a 'Carnival of the People of the North'.

1885 – The Festival opened in the month of July, the only time it has ever done so.

1887 – On June 29th and 30th the sixth Temperance Festival was held on the Town Moor. It was commented that: "the proceedings were in every way successful".

1888 – The Temperance Festival was extended to three days, with the opening day devoted to Highland Games.

1889 – The success of the Temperance Festival continued. People were brought to the event by train from places as far away as 200 miles.

"The eighth annual Temperance Festival was commenced on the Newcastle Town Moor in brilliant weather. Crowds of holiday-makers wended their way to the Moor on this and the two following days. The sports provided for the patrons were highly appreciated, while the showmen and roundabout proprietors did a thriving business. It was computed that between 100,000 and 150,000 persons were present on the second day. The festival was considered the most successful yet held."

North Country Lore & Legend, 1889

'I've got a lovely bunch of coconuts!' A coconut seller at the Temperance Festival, circa 1895. At this time, coconuts were considered to be exotic. Coconut sellers still attend the Hoppings to this day and are placed at strategic positions around the fair.

1890 – The ninth annual Festival was opened by Alderman W. D. Stephens and took the usual form of athletic and military sports, juveniles' games, and treats for poor children. As a counter-attraction, the Temperance Festival Association would have had its work cut out in drawing the crowds away from the Gosforth Park races as Prince Albert Victor, the scandal-hit grandson of Queen Victoria, was in attendance.

1891 – Alderman W. D. Stephens, President of the Festival, had his watch stolen on his way to the Moor. A new watch was bought for him in recognition of his services.

1895 – The Corporation took control over the letting of the sites, with the lessee showman having to pay £500 in rent.

1897 – William Murphy, showman and lessee, paid £775 rent. A bonfire was lit on the Cowhill during the Festival to commemorate Queen Victoria's 60 years on the throne.

1899 – John Murphy, lessee, provided shows and roundabouts at the Temperance Festival. Rent was lower this year at £735.

1900 – John Murphy paid £780 rent for the Race Week Fair. Alderman W. D. Stephens was ill and missed the Festival opening ceremony. He also missed the opening in 1901.

A stallholder shakes his wooden ratchet to draw attention to his coconut saloon at the Temperance Festival in the 1890s.

1902 – Alderman W. D. Stephens died and the press commented that it was sad that he did not live to see the 21st Festival milestone.

1903 – Thomas Hurst of Clifton, Manchester, was recorded as being lessee. The new President of the Festival Association, Mr Bainbridge, was unable to attend the opening.

1905 – The Town Moor was leased to showman George Green of Glasgow, much to the disdain of the northern showmen. George went on to establish a cinema business in his native Scotland having travelled with his own bioscope show – Green's Cinematograph.

1906 – Walker Hoadley, lessee, paid £850 for the hire of the Moor. A game of mounted pushball took place at the Festival; teams were dressed in the colours of Newcastle and Sunderland.

1907 – The North Eastern Roundabout Syndicate was formed to ensure that the Festival remained under the control of showmen from the Northern Section of the Showmen's Guild. In 1908, two tenders were submitted for the lease of the Moor: a tender of £673 from the Northern Showmen's Syndicate, comprising of Messrs James and Randall Monte Williams and Messrs Relph and Pedley; and a tender of £1,100 from the North Eastern Roundabout Proprietors Syndicate, comprising of Walker Hoadley, John, Walter and William Murphy, Harry Caris, Alfred Payne, and the Northern Stallholder's Society. The latter of the two was accepted at a meeting of the Town Moor Management.

Hoadley's gallopers and slip (helter skelter) at the Jesmond Hoppings in 1914.

1909 – The Temperance Festival Association and North of England Roundabout Proprietors Association suffered a loss in takings owing to bad weather. The Freemen and Corporation granted an extension to the Festival for the first time ever; two days were added to allow the showmen a chance to recoup their losses.

1911 – A young man was struck by lightning and killed on the Moor while watching the build up of the shows. Another unfortunate incident occurred that year; at the official opening, the podium collapsed during the speeches and several dignitaries were injured.

1912 – Mr Walker, Chairman of the Freemen's Stewards' Committee, allowed the showmen two extra days on the Moor following extreme weather which caused the fair to be suspended. Damage was caused to the Moor when the attractions left.

1913 – In May, an action was brought by the Stewards' Committee of the Freemen against John and William Murphy, Walker Hoadley, and William Pedley of the North Eastern Roundabout Syndicate (Walker v Murphy). The plaintiffs asked for an injunction to restrain the defendants from 'interfering with the turf of the Moor by placing thereon any steam engines, shoe, caravan, exhibition, booth, tent or similar thing'. The showmen lost the case and had to pay damages of £214 for the injury to the pasturage. The Festival went ahead after the order was discharged by the Appeal Court on June 20th 1913. The case was, however, later reopened and it was decided that the Corporation must have the consent of the Freemen before letting sites on the Moor to the showmen.

The smaller Hoppings fairground at Jesmond Vale, 1914. The fairground was closed at the time this photograph was taken. The large ride in the centre, with a traction engine alongside it, is a Joy Wheel.

1914 to 1918 – The Festival relocated to the Green Pool Field in Jesmond Vale for the duration of the Great War. Troops were trained on the Town Moor and parts of it were used as an airstrip. In 1915 the Festival was held in Jesmond Dene during Race Week.

1919 – The Festival returned to the Town Moor.

1920 to 1923 – The Temperance Festival did not take place on the Town Moor. Instead, smaller Hoppings took place at Jesmond Vale.

1923 – Councillor David Adams MP, the Sheriff of the City, proposed that the Temperance Festival be revived in the next year. Local businessman and friend of the showmen, Arthur Fenwick, commented: "To stop the showmen coming on to the Moor was for them just as serious a business as would be the closing of the Tyne to the shipping community."

1924 – In January the fate of the Festival was in jeopardy when the Freemen proposed that they receive two thirds of the income from the lease of the Moor. The West Newcastle Labour Party urged the City Council to allow the Festival to go ahead regardless of whether the Freemen gave consent. The situation was resolved two months later and the original terms of fifty-fifty were accepted by the Corporation and Freemen. The Revived Temperance Festival opened on the Moor on June 24th, with rent of £1,000 being paid by the lessees. At this time, the Hon Secretary of the Lost Children's Tent was Miss Doris J. Edington. Arthur Fenwick later lamented the fact that he missed the Civic Party tour as he had had to leave for the Golden Wedding celebrations of his wife's parents.

A sad day for the fair as John Walter Murphy's funeral cortege departs the Town Moor on June 30th 1931. An impressive memorial, which cost 160 Guineas, marks his grave (Con-C-10474) at Preston Cemetery in North Shields.

c1924 – George Wright became Festival Site Manager and acted on behalf of the Newcastle Corporation and the Stewards' Committee of Freemen. His responsibilities included trouble-shooter, diplomat, administrator and guardian. He was in this role for over thirty years and retired in 1956.

1925 – The cost of the North of England Temperance Festival Association's official programme was 2d.

1927 – On June 22nd, a windstorm caused chaos and damaged stalls and rides.

1929 – William Murphy was thought to be the oldest showman on the ground at the age of 72. He made mention of how his rent this year was £3,100 when in 1887 he had paid between £60 and £70 for the lease of the Moor.

1930s – Daily visitors totalled 150,000 on days of good weather.

1931 – Rent for the lessees was £3,500. John Walter Murphy, the eldest son of Walter Murphy, died while at the Town Moor; the funeral cortege departed the fairground for his internment at Preston Cemetery in North Shields. A trade section was introduced to the Temperance Festival and in later years became known as Swag Man's Alley; it is still a feature of the Hoppings today.

William Stewart's Boxing Booth on the Moor in 1933.

1932 – June 15th - Colin Noble, one of the current organisers, first visited the Fair when he was three days old.

1933 – Mrs Nellie Beatty, known as 'Ma' to the children, took charge of the Lost Children's tent and went on to provide her services at the Fair for over 30 years.

1934 – Invitations for Civic Guests to the official opening made mention that it was in commemoration of the first year of Direct Letting, which saw the Corporation and Freemen being responsible for letting the individual positions direct to the showmen. The rent to Ernest Atha for a pie and pea stall was £3 15s 0d; the rent to Mrs A. Watkins for a round game was £16 10s 0d; and rent to David Crisbone, Glasgow, for his shooting saloon was £3 0s 0d. Mr J. R. Andrews, Chairman of the Freemen, said that the new arrangements would bring in £5,500 in rent. Interestingly, this was the first year in which the showground stretched from Grandstand Road to Exhibition Park. A car park, operated by the British Legion at the north end of the Moor, was introduced.

1935 – The showmen appear to have been unhappy with the introduction of Direct Letting the year before, as an arbitration hearing took place at the County Court on Westgate Road on June 6th; Judge Thesiger found in favour of the Corporation and Freemen but, having praised the showmen for their efforts, made suggestions of definitive prices, a longer application time, and concessions with the deposits. The Town Moor Festival plan was modified to allow for the Royal Agricultural Show to take place on the Moor.

Covers of the Holidays at Home programme of events from 1942 and 1944.

1937 – Newcastle Corporation limited the number of round stalls on the Moor to one hundred and seventy five. The Official Opening took place on John Powell's brand new Speedway.

1939 – Only three out of the thirty large rides in attendance were considered of the old type, showing how the public's taste for grand and ornate rides had changed to a thirst for speed, thrills and excitement.

1940 & 1941 – The Fair did not take place on the Town Moor owing to the outbreak of World War II. Transport difficulties and lighting regulations were imposed, and many showmen were called up to the armed forces.

1942 – A 'Holidays at Home' fair was held in Exhibition Park for six weeks. It was open from 2:30pm until 10:00pm and aimed to reduce the heavy demands on road and rail transport.

1943 to 1945 – The fair, again, was housed in Exhibition Park for the rest of the War years.

1945 – October – A meeting about the reintroduction of the Town Moor Fair took place between the Corporation, the Freemen and the showmen; negotiations broke down and the showmen's offer was rejected. The Corporation proceeded to arrange its own fun fair.

An aerial view of the Town Moor Festival in the 1940s, with the Great North Road running down the left.

1946 – In April, the Corporation placed adverts in the World's Fair; the Northern Section of the Showmen's Guild recommended that its members should not attend. Only six large roundabouts, six juvenile roundabouts and a number of small stalls attended the Town Moor Fair during Race Week. A Guild fair was held at Saltwell Park, Gateshead, and proved to be the more successful of the two.

1947 – The 'Northern Syndicate of Showmen's Guild Members' was formed by Jack Murphy, William Noble Snr, Frank McConvill, Jack Hoadley and Jack Powell, and the Hoppings returned to the Town Moor. The fairground was repositioned on the Moor, running parallel to the Great North Road, because of open cast coal mining operations nearby. A heat wave, coupled with a bus strike, played havoc with the attendance. John Murphy, one of the current organisers, made his first visit to the Town Moor Fair.

1951 – The Rotor, a spinning wall ride, first featured at the Fair. Ron Taylor visited the Moor for the first time with his boxing booth. Ron took over the booth in 1936 when his father died. A children's novel, The Witch of Redesdale, was published by Newcastle author Winifred Cawley and opened with: "The whole of Tyneside seemed to be flocking towards the Moor, eager to find out what this, one of the biggest fairs in the country, had to offer them."

Alan Proudlock riding on a juvenile ride in the late 1950s.

1956 – The date of the Hoppings was brought forward a week so as not to coincide with the Royal Show; attendance figures dropped owing to bad publicity of the date change.

1957 – Edith Barlow, known as 'Little Edie', was the Shortest Woman in the World at 22 inches and weighing 17 pounds. She took ill while on the Moor and died in hospital from pneumonia at the age of 28 years. Edie was known to have smoked forty cigarettes a day. Fred Didsbury, Newcastle City Council's Chief Building Surveyor, became Fair Manager and was known to the showmen as 'The Guvnor'.

1958 – Over 200 tons of ashes were used on the ground during the week due to the wet conditions. For the first time ever, an extension of one week was granted by Newcastle Corporation in an attempt to prevent damage to the Moor occurring. A Hook-the-Duck appeared at the Hoppings for the first time.

1959 – Albert Austin assisted Fred Didsbury with the setting out of the fairground for the first time, having gained employment with the Council as a Building Inspector the year before.

1960 – Owing to the dry weather 1,500 gallons of water were used on the south entrance area and the car park entrance to dampen dust. This proved unsuccessful and produced muddy conditions.

Codona's Waltzer at the Hoppings, circa 1965. The ride was built in 1962 by George Maxwell of Edinburgh and can now be seen in an amusement park in Aberdeen.

1962 – The presence of the Royal Agricultural Show saw the Hoppings being sited further north on the Moor. On June 24th, a 70 mph gale forced emergency measures to be taken in the early morning; heavy vehicles were placed around the machines to act as wind breaks. Debris and material from the Royal Show, and in particular a corrugated steel dome, landed on the ground and wrecked one of the showmen's stalls.

1963 – The Hoppings was extended due to the non-stop rain.

1964 – Around 200 lost children were reported during the week. It is thought that many were getting lost on purpose to cash in on the free sweets which were given to the found children.

1965 – Mrs Beatty, the lady in charge of the lost children's tent, was unable to attend the fair due to ill health.

1967 – The Hoppings was held a week late as the Jockey Club had changed the Newcastle Race Week dates so as not to clash with the Royal Ascot Meeting.

1969 – 400,000 gallons of water had to be pumped out of the Lakeland area to stop the continual overflow across the Moor, south of Forsyth path.

A Fun House on the Moor in the 1970s. This type of attraction has increased in popularity – and in size – with several multi-storey versions visiting the Hoppings in 2009.

1970 – Rent was reported to be £6,000.

1971 – Rent was reported to be £8,500. A licence was granted to include an extra day, allowing the showmen to open on the Friday night as compensation for the increase in rent. At this time, the cost of having your palm read was 50p or 60p.

1972 – Rent to the showmen was reported as £7,500, double the rent of the 1950s.

1975 – The Hoppings opened for the first time on a Sunday (2pm – 8pm), amid objections from a minority of Sabbatarians. There was no longer a Speakers' Corner on the Moor, which had been a popular feature of earlier Festivals.

1977 – The Evening Chronicle reported a 15% increase in the rent since 1975, now at £14,500. 72 year old Gilbert Chadwick, novelty freak show proprietor, said in the press that this year would be his last Hoppings, having first visited with his show in 1934 when admission was 2d for children and 3d for adults.

1978 – The Official Opening took place on the track of Billy Crow's dodgems owing to the absence of the usual official podium.

Town Moor Festival Centenary
1882 - 1982
A Short History of the Newcastle upon Tyne
Town Moor Temperance Festival

THE Newcastle upon Tyne Town Moor Festival was founded in 1882 by Alderman W.D. Stephens and eleven bearded and bewhiskered patriarchs, as a counter-attraction to the Summer Race Meeting at Gosforth Park — these two events always being held annually during the last complete week in June.

From 1721 to 1881 the Race Meetings had been held on the Moor attended by strolling players with their booths, including that Northern celebrity, Billy Purvis, the famous Newcastle clown, but even previous to this, in the time of Charles 1st the horses ran on the Town Moor, after which the races were transferred to Killingworth for some years.

The first Festival lasted only two days and the rent paid by the Showmen was said to be only £10, but now this great gathering of Travelling Shows, having from time to time been extended, lasts seven days, from the Saturday preceding the Race holidays to the end of the following week. The Showmen have to pay in the neighbourhood of £5,000 rent for these few days on the Moor, which for many years was not so many hundred, in fact I can remember Granny Murphy boasting that her family first leased the space for the Shows on the Town Moor from the City Authorities for £70. (June 1939).

The commemorative envelope produced for the Centenary Hoppings in 1982.

1979 – Frank Baron, a police inspector stationed at Gosforth, became responsible for policing the fair. He continued until 1982 and two years later published a diary-format book on the history of the Hoppings. Ron Taylor's boxing booth was wrecked in a road crash. This year Ron presented a helter skelter (known as a slip to showpeople) and said he was "broken hearted" at not having his booth on the Moor.

1980 – The Hoppings was struck by hailstones, thunder, lightning and torrential rain. Ron Taylor's boxing booth opened for the last three days of the fair, the paintwork having just been finished by artist Paul Wright, who worked under the mercy of the inclement weather.

1981 – Rent was reported to be £30,000.

1982 – The Hoppings celebrated its 100th anniversary. Commemorative envelopes with special stamps were sold at £1 each, and copies of the original Temperance Festival programme cover were sold for 75p each. A heritage display was hosted by the Central Library. Unfortunately poor weather blighted the centenary Hoppings. This was Fred Didsbury's last Hoppings and he retired from the Council the following April. William H. Tait, known as Bill, of Bedlington succeeded him as Fair Manager. When asked how he regarded the fair he said it was the low point of his year!

A general view of the fairground in the 1980s. The four rides in the background are: The Zipper; The Skyliner (also known as the American Eggs); the Dive Bombers; and Murphy's Waltzer.

c1983 – Free fairground outings for underprivileged children commenced in a small way. By 1986 around 3,000 Variety Club children were attending the Hoppings, with all rides donated by the Showmen's Guild. This was the last year in which goldfish were offered as prizes at the Hoppings.

1985 – Attendance dipped below 100,000 as the recession hit. A proposal to merge the Hoppings with the Tyneside Summer Exhibition was rejected by the City Council.

1986 – The Freemen reported that around 595 unauthorised caravans and vehicles belonging to itinerants had gained access to the Moor, a problem which had started in 1964.

1987 – The Freemen hired security guards to turn away itinerants without official passes. The Evening Chronicle reported that those turned away had set up camp in the West End of the City.

1988 – Albert Austin became Fair Manager upon his appointment as Newcastle's Chief Building Surveyor. The Town Moor Fair School was founded by teacher Maureen Bowman, when she asked Albert if she could come for an hour to mark the showchildren's work. The school went from strength to strength and soon became an established part of the Hoppings. A security system was introduced around the Town Moor to keep out itinerants who were plaguing the fairground.

Colin Noble, fifth from left, leads the Lord Mayor of Newcastle and civic guests on a tour of the fairground at the Hoppings in 1991.

1989 – The Showmen's Guild centenary was celebrated at the Hoppings with an impressive floral display at the Forsyth Road entrance. A crew filmed the Hoppings for a documentary called 'After the Lights Go Out', a behind the scenes look at the travelling community. This year marked the last appearance of a Wall of Death on the Moor until James Messham & Sons' visit in 2008.

1990 – The Hoppings was at risk of being cancelled as the controversy over the squatting itinerants continued. It was proposed that the date of the Hoppings be changed to coincide with Appleby Horse Fair so as to reduce the number of unauthorised visitors not connected to the Hoppings.

1991 – The City's Town Moor Management Committee, made up of representatives of the Council and Freemen, had expected to make just over £17,000 profit from the Hoppings, but actually made £35,359 as a result of reduced policing costs and greater use of the Hoppings car park.

1992 – The fairground went ahead regardless of sensational headlines claiming that the Hoppings could be banned because of the itinerants. A model galloping horse was presented to the Lord Mayor of Newcastle, Councillor C. A. Cook, by John Murphy and Colin Noble and is still on display in the Mayor's Silver Gallery at the Civic Centre.

The Lord Mayor of Newcastle, Councillor Joan Lamb, with Albert Austin, in 1993. This was Albert's last Hoppings as Fair Manager.

1993 – Albert Austin was made redundant from the City Council following a departmental reorganisation which saw the responsibility for the Hoppings pass from the City Engineer's Department to the Leisure Services Department. Susan Stokel-Walker became Fair Manager. Sue came to the UK from Arkansas, USA, in 1977 and is the only female Fair Manager in the history of the Hoppings. Sue shadowed Albert in his final year as Manager, but he continued to be involved with the fair - he was hired as the Fairground Surveyor.

1995 – Ron Taylor's boxing booth visited the Hoppings for the last time. A demonstration took place on the Moor to promote a Charter of Rights for fairground workers. Over 300 people attended the civil rights event and signed a petition which called for better status and less discrimination, better access to education, and parity with European showmen. One of the largest travelling wheels made an appearance at the Hoppings for the first time.

1996 – Albert Austin was approached by the Northern Syndicate and became the administrator responsible for the Syndicate's sub-leasing arrangements for the fair.

1997 – Severe weather turned the Town Moor into a quagmire. The Journal newspaper reported the cost of repair to the Moor as £30,000.

1998 – The Hoppings was postponed for a week to prevent a similar situation as the previous year from occurring.

James Mellors' aptly named Big Ben Tower. Riders are shot 42 metres into the air and back down again at 20 metres per second.

1999 – The Town Moor Fair School was organised by Alisdair MacKenzie, Education Welfare Officer, and a Newcastle teacher. Diane Barlow got involved as a traveller teacher from Northumberland.

2000 – Discussions between Valerie Moody and the Newcastle Local Education Authority led to Diane Barlow being asked to be Project Organiser for the Town Moor Fair School with Celia Datta, the Newcastle temporary traveller teacher. The school took on the theme of 'Myths and Monsters'.

2001 – Foot and mouth restrictions across the country led to many fairs being cancelled but fortunately the Hoppings went ahead. Big Ben Tower and the Bomber first featured at the Hoppings. The Fair School was organised by John Braithwaite and Diane Barlow.

2002 – The 120th anniversary Hoppings started on Friday, June 21st and ran until Sunday, June 30th. The Lord Mayor of Newcastle, Councillor John Marshall, officially opened the fairground, which had three full sized rollercoasters in attendance. This was a year of record numbers; the Hoppings had almost one million visitors and police records showed that crime and arrests had gone down from 2001. Diane Barlow made modifications to the organisation of the Town Moor Fair School, as attendance had increased with lots of younger pupils. Extra help was provided by volunteers from Northumbria University and Gosforth High School.

Abie Danter's Jungle River log flume in 2005. The ride was made by French ride manufacturer Reverchon in 2001.

2003 – A 30 ft silver and blue sculpture was unveiled at the Hoppings by artist Boris Howarth. The artwork, which was shaped like a triple helix, was erected as a gateway to the fairground. 'Ginger' Johnny Brown celebrated his fortieth year on Keith Turner & Sons' Imperial Waltzer. A surprise presentation was made to him on the Moor. John Braithwaite and Diane Barlow organised the Fair School. Paul Lanagan first visited the school as part of his research for a Town Moor Fair book, but ended up returning each year with greater involvement.

2004 – Councillor Margaret Carter opened the Hoppings for the second time and became the only Lord Mayor in the history of the Hoppings to have done so, when her term of office was extended to allow the local elections to take place on the same day as a European election. Supply Teacher Bob Day got involved with the Fair School and introduced more physical and practical activities to the proceedings.

2005 – Murphy's Waltzer returned to the Hoppings for the first time since 1982. Diane Barlow retired as organiser of the Fair School.

2006 – Showman Keith James almost missed the Hoppings when his fair permits ended up 18,000 miles away in Papua New Guinea instead of Selston, Nottinghamshire. England playing in the World Cup quarterfinal had an effect on the fair – many showmen could be seen watching televisions in their roundstalls. Sarah Edgar, from Newcastle Ethnic Minority, Traveller & Refugee Achievement Service, became teacher in charge of the Town Moor Fair School.

Albert Austin, left, is presented with a silver salver from showman John Murphy in 2008. The ornate tray was engraved with the words: 'Albert Austin, in recognition of long and outstanding service, from the Northern Syndicate.'

2007 – This year's Hoppings was regarded by some as being the worst in living memory. Powerful tractors with treaded wheels had to be used to drag the attractions out of the mud. The repair of the damaged Moor was reported in the press to have cost over £50,000, and it was even suggested that the Moor needed a year off from the event! Peter Scott, Recreational Development Officer, started to shadow Susan Stokel-Walker, Fair Manager, as the City Council's onsite representative.

2008 – A bond of a substantial amount was paid by the showmen in advance of the Hoppings to ensure the cost of any potential damage to the Moor was covered. A food kiosk at the lower end of the Moor caught fire; during the official opening members of the Civic Party could see the plume of smoke from the top end of the Moor. Police praised the good nature shown by the tens of thousands of attendees to this year's fair, as only minor incidents occurred, with the police handing out 48-hour ban notices to only six people who were deemed too drunk to participate. Showfamilies from the Hoppings raised £2,300 for the Sir Bobby Robson Foundation at a social event in Newcastle. Albert Austin retired from his role as Fairground Surveyor owing to the City Council's policy of not employing anyone over the age of 75. A surprise afternoon tea, arranged by Susan Stokel-Walker, was hosted by the Lord and Lady Mayoress of Newcastle at the Mansion House, Jesmond, on September 6th, in recognition of Albert's services to the Hoppings. A severe downpour occurred on the day – true Hoppings weather – and many of the City's roads were flooded out.

Albert Austin shortly after his surprise presentation of honorary life membership of the Showmen's Guild at the Hoppings in 2009. Pictured above are, from left: Jimmy Williams, National President of the Guild; Maureen Austin; Arthur Robert Moody, Chairman of the Northern Section of the Guild; Albert Austin; John Murphy and Colin Noble; and the Lord Mayor of Newcastle.

2009 – As a precaution, extra fertiliser was added to the grass on the Moor to ensure it was longer and thicker prior to the fair's arrival. After the Hoppings was officially opened by the Lord Mayor of Newcastle, Albert Austin was surprised with a presentation of honorary life membership of the Showmen's Guild of Great Britain and was given an ornate model traction engine which featured the words: 'Mighty in Strength and Endurance'. Later in the week, the children from the Town Moor Fair School presented Albert with a handmade card congratulating him on becoming a showman! The news of the death of pop star Michael Jackson broke on the Moor and many of the rides could be heard playing his greatest hits. The Lord Mayor of Newcastle, Councillor Michael Cookson, visited the Fair School and gave out certificates to the children on the last Friday. Later in the year, on November 24th, he hosted a tea party at the Civic Centre as a thank you for all the organisers and volunteers from the school.

To be continued...

At the 2009 Hoppings, Bart and Homer Simpson made a series of special guest appearances, as did kiddies' favourite Bob the Builder.

The Lord Mayor of Newcastle, Councillor Michael Cookson, in his chamber with Valerie Moody M.B.E., at a special thank you tea for the organisers of the Town Moor Fair School, 2009.

BIBLIOGRAPHY

Publications

The Town Moor Hoppings by Frank Barron;
Newcastle: A Short History & Guide by Frank Graham;
Fairs & Shows, Newspaper Cuttings, collected by Newcastle Central Library;
Travelling Fairs by Stephen Smith, March 27th 1983;
North Country Lore & Legend;
Geographical Magazine;
A Short History of Newcastle upon Tyne Town Moor Temperance Festival by Arthur Fenwick.

Newspapers

The World's Fair;
The Evening Chronicle;
The Journal;
The Illustrated London News;
The Guardian.

Photo Credits

Paul Lanagan Collection: 4a, 5a, 12a, 13a, 14b, 15a, 15b, 16a, 17a, 17b, 18a, 18b, 18c, 19a, 19b, 20a, 21b, 23b, 26a, 27b, 28a, 32b, 33a, 34a, 34b, 35b, 36b, 37a, 37b, 39b, 40b, 41a, 41b, 42b, 43a, 43b, 45a, 45b, 46a, 46b, 50a, 50b, 51a, 52b, 53a, 53b, 54b, 55a, 56b, 57b, 58a, 59a, 59b, 60a, 61a, 62a, 62b, 63a, 64a, 64b, 66a, 66b, 67a, 67b, 68a, 68b, 69a, 69b, 70a, 70b, 71a, 71b, 72a, 75a, 75b, 75c, 75d, 75e, 77a, 83b, 85b, 86a, 86b, 87a, 87b, 88a, 88b, 89a, 91b, 93b, 94a, 94b, 95a, 95b, 96b, 97a, 97b, 106a, 106b, 107a, 107b, 108a, 108b, 109a, 109b, 110a, 110b, 111a, 111b, 112a, 112b, 131a, 132a, 133a, 134a, 135a, and 135b.

National Fairground Archive: 2a, 11a, 26b, 27a, 29a, 30b, 31a, 31b, 32a, 35a, 38a, 38b, 39a, 47a, 48a, 48b, 57a, 73a, 76a, 81a, 90a, 90b, 118a, 121a, 125a, and 136c.

Thomas Dixon Collection: 20b, 21a, 23a, 42a, 44a, 56a, 65a, 80a, 80b, 81b, 85a, 99a, 104a, 120a, 122a, 122b, 126a, 127a, and 127b.

Ward Phillipson Collection: 113a, 115a, 117a, 136a, and 136b.

Newcastle City Library: 114a, 116a, and 119a.

Tyne & Wear Archive Service: 8a, and 9a.

H. S. Thorne: 7a, and 49b.

If you have any photographs of the Hoppings fairground which you would like to share, please contact the author at: info@newcastle-hoppings.co.uk